English
for
Academic
Study:

Pronunciation

Study Book

Jonathan Smith and Annette Margolis

University of Reading

Centre for Applied Language Studies

Garnet EDUCATION

Credits

Published by
Garnet Publishing Ltd.
8 Southern Court
South Street
Reading RG1 4QS, UK

First edition 2007
Reprinted 2008
Fully revised 2009

ISBN: 978 1 85964 487 4

British Library Cataloguing-in-Publication Data
A catalogue record for this book is available from the
British Library.

Production
Project manager:	Simone Davies
Project consultant:	Rod Webb
Editorial team:	Penny Analytis, Emily Clarke, James Croft, Fiona McGarry, Richard Peacock
Art director:	Mike Hinks
Design and layout:	Nick Asher
Illustration:	Nick Asher
Photography:	Corbis; David Lyons/Alamy; Jonathan Smith
Audio:	Matinée Sound and Vision

Printed and bound
in Great Britain by Cambrian Printers Ltd,
Aberystwyth, Wales

Contents

Book map

	Topic	Objectives
1	• Vowel sounds: /æ/, /e/, /ɪ/, /ɑː/, /ɜː/, /iː/ • Syllables and word stress • Weak forms in function words	• Learn which phonemic symbols represent certain vowel sounds • Practise recognizing and producing these vowel sounds • Learn about the concepts of the syllable and word stress • Practise producing words with the correct word stress • Practise recognizing weak forms of function words when listening
2	• Vowel sounds: /ɒ/, /ʌ/, /ə/, /ʊ/, /ɔː/, /uː/ • Unstressed syllables and word stress patterns	• Learn which phonemic symbols represent the other vowel sounds • Practise recognizing and producing these vowel sounds • Learn more about which syllable is stressed in some types of word
3	• Voiced and unvoiced consonants • Consonant sounds: /θ/, /ð/, /t/, /s/ • Sentence stress	• Learn about the pronunciation of voiced and unvoiced consonants • Practise recognizing and producing these sounds • Learn to identify stressed words in sentences • Practise using sentence stress to highlight important information
4	• Consonant sounds: /ʒ/, /v/, /j/, /ʃ/, /tʃ/, /dʒ/ • Word stress on two-syllable words	• Learn more phonemic symbols representing consonant sounds • Practise recognizing and producing these consonant sounds • Learn where to place the stress in words with two syllables
5	• Diphthongs: /aɪ/, /əʊ/, /eɪ/ • Sounds in connected speech: linking, insertion	• Learn which phonemic symbols represent certain diphthongs • Practise recognizing and producing diphthongs • Learn how the pronunciation of words is affected by their context in connected speech
6	• Consonant clusters: at the beginning and in the middle of words • Sounds in connected speech: disappearing sounds, contractions • Tone units	• Learn how to pronounce groups of consonants (consonant clusters) at the beginning and in the middle of words • Learn how to divide up connected speech into tone units
7	• Diphthongs: /aʊ/, /eə/, /ɪə/, /ɔɪ/ • Sentence stress and tone units	• Learn which phonemic symbols represent other diphthongs • Practise recognizing and producing these diphthongs • Have more practice identifying sentence stress and tone units
8	• Consonant clusters: at the end of words and across two words • Intonation	• Learn how to pronounce consonant clusters at the end of words and across two words • Learn how intonation is used to organize and emphasize information

Introduction

EAS: Pronunciation has been designed with the aims of helping you to:
- improve the accuracy of your pronunciation;
- develop your listening micro-skills;
- learn the phonemic alphabet;
- build your understanding of sound/spelling relationships;
- recognize and remember words and phrases that commonly occur in academic contexts.

Accuracy of pronunciation

Accurate pronunciation is important if you want people to understand you clearly. Frequent pronunciation errors may put a strain on the listener, and may also lead to breakdowns in communication. While you do not have to speak with a perfect English accent, your aim must be at least for your pronunciation to be good enough for the listener to understand you with ease. The main technique you can use to achieve this is to listen and repeat patterns of pronunciation, but learning the phonemic alphabet and developing a sensitive ear will also help you. If you are using this book with a teacher, his or her feedback will help you to identify which aspects of pronunciation you need to focus on, and what progress you are making in improving your pronunciation.

Learning the phonemic alphabet

The phonemic alphabet is a system for showing the pronunciation of words in English, and is shown on page 7 of this book. At first glance, the phonemic alphabet looks like another language that you have to learn. However, about half of the 44 phonemic symbols that you are expected to know are pronounced in the same way as they are written. In *EAS: Pronunciation* we have focused on:

- those <u>symbols</u> which may be unfamiliar, and so may be difficult to learn;
- those <u>sounds</u> which may be difficult to pronounce for certain learners.

We believe that learning the phonemic alphabet will help you to develop more accurate pronunciation and improve your listening skills. In addition, if you know the phonemic alphabet you can:

- understand the correct pronunciation when looking up a word in a dictionary;
- note down the correct pronunciation in your vocabulary notebook.

So, knowing the phonemic alphabet is another important aspect of recording and learning vocabulary.

Listening micro-skills

In listening classes, you will have had practice understanding meaning that is built up over a sentence or several sentences, but you may have had difficulty with comprehension at a lower level. Listening micro-skills are the skills you need to understand meaning at the level of a word or small group of words.

Students frequently remark that there are many words that they know in their written form, but fail to recognize when listening. There may be several reasons for this; for example, words may not be pronounced in the way you expect them to be, or it may be difficult to hear where one word ends and another begins. Many activities in this book will help you to deal with such problems.

Sound/spelling relationships

Another difficulty faced by students is that there does not seem to be a relationship between the way words are spelt in English and the way they are pronounced. This creates problems, not just for accurate pronunciation, but also for correct spelling. In fact, while there are exceptions (and many of these exceptions seem to relate to the most common words in English), there are a lot of useful sound/spelling patterns. If you can ensure that you are familiar with these patterns, you can then focus on learning the exceptions, which are the words that create the most problems.

Academic vocabulary

The examples and exercises in these materials are focused on words from:

- the General Service List (GSL): the 2,000 most frequently used words in English;
- the Academic Word List (AWL): a list of 570 word families that are most commonly used in academic contexts.

All the words in the AWL will be useful to you, but some of the words in the GSL are either words you may know already (e.g., *you*, *from*, *hand*) or words that are not commonly or widely used in academic contexts (e.g., *handkerchief*, *niece*, *jealous*). In general, words like these have not been used in the examples and exercises.

In addition, a number of extracts from academic lectures have been used to provide practice in listening for features of pronunciation.

A lot of care has been taken, therefore, to ensure that the vocabulary focused on in this book is relevant to both academic study and your needs. Many words will be those you 'half know', so the materials should reinforce your understanding. Other words may be quite new to you.

Using the materials

There is a range of different exercises which require you to work in different ways. For example, you may need to:

- listen and repeat words or sentences;
- stop the recording and read an explanation;
- stop the recording, write words in spaces in sentences, then listen to check your answers;
- stop the recording, fill in a table or choose the correct answer, then listen to check your answers.

If you just play the recording non-stop, listening and reading at the same time, you will not improve your pronunciation or listening skills. You will have to stop the recording to read, think, write and check answers, and you will have to replay short sections you have difficulty with.

Recording your own voice

When you are asked to listen and repeat words, phrases or sentences, it can also be very useful to record your own voice and then play it back. This will enable you to compare your own pronunciation with the recording, and hear any differences or problems clearly. You will not need to record your voice for every exercise, but try to do this when you know you have a problem with certain aspects of pronunciation.

If you are unsure whether your pronunciation on an exercise is accurate enough, and you are working with a teacher, ask him or her to listen to your recording. He or she will be able to assess your pronunciation more objectively.

Phonemic alphabet

Consonants							
/p/	/t/	/k/	/s/	/ʃ/	/tʃ/	/f/	/θ/
post	take	keep	snow	shoe	choice	leaf	thin
/b/	/d/	/g/	/z/	/ʒ/	/dʒ/	/v/	/ð/
book	doctor	goal	zero	measure	jump	leave	the
/h/	/m/	/n/	/ŋ/	/l/	/r/	/w/	/j/
hotel	meet	nine	bring	late	red	well	yes

Vowels					
/æ/	/e/	/ɪ/	/ɒ/	/ʌ/	/ə/
plan	end	big	job	sum	the
/ʊ/	/ɑː/	/ɜː/	/iː/	/ɔː/	/uː/
good	car	her	fee	law	too

Diphthongs							
/aɪ/	/aʊ/	/əʊ/	/eɪ/	/eə/	/ɪə/	/ɔɪ/	/ʊə/
why	now	go	day	care	dear	enjoy	pure

Notes:

1. The sound /ə/ is very common in unstressed syllables in English.
   In this sentence it occurs seven times: *Poverty is at the centre of the problem.*

2. The sound /ʊə/ is relatively uncommon in English.

3. Many vowel or diphthong sounds can be spelt in different ways, e.g., /ɜː/ in *her, turn, heard, word,* and many similar spellings can be pronounced in different ways, e.g., *head* /hed/, *heat* /hiːt/, *heart* /hɑːt/, *heard* /hɜːd/.

Vowel sounds 1, word stress and weak forms

In this unit you will:
- learn which phonemic symbols represent certain vowel sounds;
- practise recognizing and producing these vowel sounds;
- learn about the concepts of the syllable and word stress;
- practise producing words with the correct word stress;
- practise recognizing weak forms of function words when listening.

These are the 12 vowel sounds in English. In this unit, we will focus on the six sounds shaded in this table.

/æ/	/e/	/ɪ/	/ɒ/	/ʌ/	/ə/
pl<u>a</u>n	<u>e</u>nd	b<u>ig</u>	j<u>o</u>b	s<u>u</u>m	th<u>e</u>
/ʊ/	/ɑː/	/ɜː/	/iː/	/ɔː/	/uː/
g<u>oo</u>d	c<u>ar</u>	h<u>er</u>	f<u>ee</u>	l<u>aw</u>	t<u>oo</u>

Task 1: Vowel sounds

1.1 🎧 **CD1 – 1 Listen to the difference in the pronunciation of these pairs of words. In each of them, the vowel sound is different.**

a)	/ɪ/	/iː/		**c)**	/æ/	/ɑː/
	fit	feet			hat	heart
	dip	deep			match	march
	hit	heat			pack	park

b)	/æ/	/e/		**d)**	/e/	/ɜː/
	mass	mess			ten	turn
	band	bend			head	heard
	had	head			went	weren't

Listen again and repeat the words.

1.2 🎧 **CD1 – 2 You will hear some of the words from Ex 1.1. Listen and circle the phonemic transcription that matches the pronunciation of the word you hear.**

Example: /hed/ ⟨/hɜːd/⟩

a)	/pæk/	/pɑːk/		**f)**	/dɪp/	/diːp/
b)	/ten/	/tɜːn/		**g)**	/hæd/	/hed/
c)	/mæs/	/mes/		**h)**	/hæt/	/hɑːt/
d)	/hɪt/	/hiːt/		**i)**	/bænd/	/bend/
e)	/went/	/wɜːnt/				

1.3 🎧 **CD1 – 3 Listen to six more words and do the following exercises.**

a) Listen and circle the phonemic transcription that matches the pronunciation of the word you hear.

1 /sɪt/	_____	/siːt/	_____
2 /mæt/	_____	/met/	_____
3 /hɜːt/	_____	/hɑːt/	_____
4 /fɑː/	_____	/fɜː/	_____
5 /lɪv/	_____	/liːv/	_____
6 /sæd/	_____	/sed/	_____

b) Write the words, with the correct spelling, in the spaces next to the phonemic transcriptions.

Task 2: Syllables

For pronunciation purposes, words can be divided into syllables. A syllable contains only one vowel sound, which may be preceded or followed by consonants. Remember that some consonants are pronounced as vowels; for example, *heavy* is a two-syllable word, because the *y* is pronounced as a vowel.

2.1 🎧 **CD1 – 4 Listen to these examples of words with one, two and three or more syllables.**

a) one-syllable words

> aid   quote   source   fee

b) two-syllable words

> cred•it   ac•cept   heav•y   e•quate

c) words with three or more syllables

> pol•i•cy (3)   sim•i•lar (3)   en•vi•ron•ment (4)   i•den•ti•fy (4)   in•di•vid•ual (4)

2.2 🎧 **CD1 – 5 Listen to these words and decide how many syllables there are in each of them.**

	Syllables			Syllables
a) specific	_____	**f)**	consequent	_____
b) alter	_____	**g)**	framework	_____
c) resource	_____	**h)**	significant	_____
d) preliminary	_____	**i)**	adapt	_____
e) available	_____	**j)**	differentiate	_____

Pronunciation note

There is some variation in the way people pronounce words. For example, some people pronounce *preliminary* with four syllables – /prɪˈlɪmɪnrɪ/, while other people pronounce it with five syllables – /prɪˈlɪmɪnərɪ/.

Task 3: Word stress patterns

In words of more than one syllable, one syllable is emphasized more than others; it has a stronger sound than other syllables.

3.1 🎧 **CD1 – 6 Listen for the stressed syllable in these words.**
The stressed syllable is marked with (').

> 'pol•i•cy   'sim•i•lar   en•'vi•ron•ment   i•'den•ti•fy   in•di•'vid•ual
> as•'sume   'ma•jor   o•ver•'seas   op•e•'ra•tion   re•in•'force

3.2 🎧 **CD1 – 7 Listen again to the words from Ex 2.2. Mark the stressed syllables as shown in the following example.**

Example: a) spe'cific

3.3 🎧 **CD1 – 8 Listen to the following sentences and mark the stressed syllable in the words in bold.**

a) The **protection** of children is the main **purpose** of this legislation.

b) The samples were **analyzed** in the lab.

c) Chemical **analysis** of the rock provided surprising results.

d) The aim of the study was to **identify** the **factors** contributing to domestic violence.

e) **Periodicals** are kept in an area on the ground floor.

f) The **administration** of these drugs needs to be closely monitored.

g) In **percentage** terms, this is not a significant increase.

h) This is the standard **procedure** for limiting spread of the disease.

Task 4: Strong and weak forms of function words

4.1 🎧 **CD1 – 9 Listen to these pairs of sentences. What is the difference in the pronunciation of the words in bold in each pair? How can you explain this difference?**

a) 1 Interest rates **are** rising.
    2 No, that's not true. We **are** doing something about it.

b) 1 Would you like **some** tea?
    2 Most scientists are convinced about global warming, but **some** are not.

c) 1 Where's he coming **from**?
    2 Results differed **from** one region to another.

d) 1 Is that **your** pen or mine?
    2 Can I borrow **your** dictionary?

Pronunciation note

Ex 4.1 shows that the pronunciation of some one-syllable function words may be different when these words are *unstressed* (or *weak*) in a sentence, compared with their pronunciation when they are *stressed* (or *strong*). Function words are very common words (including conjunctions, pronouns, prepositions, articles, determiners and auxiliary and modal verbs) that do not seem to have much meaning, but are used to show relationships between vocabulary words or to modify their meaning. Very often, the vowel sound in unstressed function words is /ə/.

In the sentences in Ex 4.1, you will see that function words are *stressed* when they *add emphasis*, e.g., *No, that's not true. We **are** doing something about it*. This is also done to *indicate a contrast*, e.g., *Most scientists are convinced..., but **some** are not*. You may also notice that function words at the end of sentences or questions have a strong form.

Here are some examples of these function words and their different pronunciations.

	Stressed/Strong	Unstressed/Weak
but	/bʌt/	/bət/
than	/ðæn/	/ðən/
them	/ðem/	/ðəm/
you	/juː/	/jə/
at	/æt/	/ət/
for	/fɔː/	/fə/
the	/ðiː/	/ðə/
some	/sʌm/	/səm/
has	/hæz/	/həz/, /əz/
does	/dʌz/	/dəz/
can	/kæn/	/kən/

4.2 ⊙ **CD1 – 10 Listen to these sentences and write in the missing words, which are all weak forms of function words.**

a) One criticism levelled _____ the board was their lack _____ financial control.

b) This issue was discussed _____ some length during the conference.

c) These points should _____ been made more effectively.

d) How do we account _____ this change in behaviour?

e) This might do more harm _____ good.

f) This kind of restructuring is usually regarded by employees _____ a change _____ the worse.

g) This problem _____ easily be solved _____ minimal cost.

h) Trade sanctions will be imposed with effect from the 1st _____ December.

4.3 CD1 – 11 **Study the following introduction to a lecture on globalization. Then listen and write in the missing words, which again are weak forms of function words.**

Well, as Ros said, I'm going to talk about globalization today, which is one _____ the catch phrases or buzzwords, if you like, _____ the late 20th _____ early 21st centuries. It's constantly in _____ news. It's used by politicians, by people in _____ media, by business people, and when they're referring _____ globalization they talk about things like _____ way we _____ communicate almost instantaneously nowadays with people on the other side _____ _____ world by e-mail or by television. They're also talking about, _____ example, the way that _____ fall in share prices in one part _____ _____ world, _____ example in the Far East, _____ have an immediate impact on the stock markets on the other side _____ _____ world, like in London _____ Frankfurt.

4.4 CD1 – 12 **Listen to these phrases and repeat them. Can you identify and produce the weak forms of the function words?**

a) past and present figures

b) more or less fifty

c) they were selected at random

d) it was far from clear

e) the results of the trials

f) too good to be true

g) needless to say

h) it's gone from bad to worse

i) we'll have to wait and see

j) we had some problems

Unit Summary

In this unit, you have learnt six English vowel sounds: /ɪ/, /iː/, /e/, /ɜː/, /æ/, /ɑː/, and practised their pronunciation. You have also become more aware of syllables and word stress, and practised listening for weak forms of function words.

1 **Say the words in the box aloud. Decide how many syllables there are in each word and write them in the correct spaces below.**

> globalization   century   constantly   politician   refer   media   financial   market

a) two-syllable words: _____ _____

b) three-syllable words: _____ _____ _____ _____

c) four-syllable words: _____

d) five-syllable words: _____

2 **CD1 – 13 Now listen to the words from Ex 1 and mark the stressed syllable in each word.**

3 **Which of the stressed syllables from Ex 2 have the following vowel sounds?**

Note: Only six of the words contain these sounds.

/ɪ/,   /iː/,   /e/,   /ɜː/,   /æ/,   /ɑː/

4 **Which words in these sentences would usually be pronounced using a weak form?**

a) Globalization is one of the buzzwords of the twenty-first century.

b) It's constantly in the news and is often referred to by politicians and the media.

c) A fall in share prices in one part of the world can have an impact on the stock markets on the other side of the world.

5 **Think about the questions below.**

a) Why do you think learners confuse some of the vowel sounds you have practised in this unit?

b) Why is it useful to note the stressed syllable when you learn a new multi-syllable word?

c) How can you check the correct stress and number of syllables of words you learn?

> For web resources, see:
>
> **www.englishforacademicstudy.com/student/pronunciation/links**
>
> These weblinks will provide you with further practice in areas of pronunciation such as the sounds, stress and intonation patterns of English.

2 Vowel sounds 2, word stress patterns

In this unit you will:
- learn which phonemic symbols represent the other vowel sounds;
- practise recognizing and producing these vowel sounds;
- learn more about which syllable is stressed in some types of word.

In Unit 1, we looked at six vowel sounds. In this unit, we will focus on the other six vowel sounds shaded in this table.

/æ/	/e/	/ɪ/	/ɒ/	/ʌ/	/ə/
plan	end	big	job	sum	the
/ʊ/	/ɑː/	/ɜː/	/iː/	/ɔː/	/uː/
good	car	her	fee	law	too

Task 1: Vowel sounds

1.1 ⊙ CD1 – 14 **Listen to the difference in the pronunciation of these pairs of words. In each of them, the vowel sound is different.**

a) /æ/

match
lack
ankle

The mouth is relaxed and quite wide open. The sound comes from the front of the mouth.

/ʌ/

much
luck
uncle

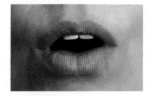

The mouth is open and slightly rounded. The sound comes from the middle of the mouth.

b) /ʊ/

pull
soot
full

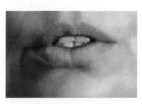

The lips are slightly rounded and pushed forwards. The sound comes from between the middle and the back of the mouth.

/uː/

pool
suit
fool

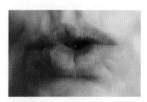

The lips are rounded and pushed forwards. The sound comes from the back of the mouth.

c) /ɒ/

spot
shot
stock

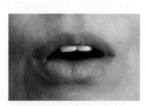

The mouth is slightly rounded and quite open. The sound comes from the back of the mouth.

/ɔː/

sport
short
stalk

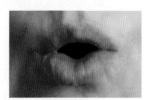

The mouth is rounded and the lips are pushed forward. The tongue is near the roof of the mouth and the sound comes from the back of the mouth.

d) /ɒ/   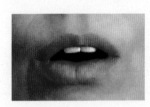   /ʊ/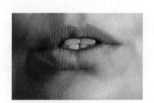

lock   look

box   books

shock   shook

Listen again and repeat the words.

1.2   🎧 **CD1 – 15 You will hear some of the words from Ex 1.1. Listen and circle the phonemic transcription that matches the pronunciation of the word you hear.**

Example: (/læk/) /lʌk/

a)	/bɒks/	/bʊks/	f)	/fʊl/	/fuːl/
b)	/pʊl/	/puːl/	g)	/lɒk/	/lʌk/
c)	/spɒt/	/spɪt/	h)	/stɒk/	/stɔːk/
d)	/mætʃ/	/mʌtʃ/	i)	/ʃɒt/	/ʃɔːt/
e)	/ænkəl/	/ʌnkəl/			

1.3   🎧 **CD1 – 16 Listen to six more words and do the following exercises.**

a) Listen and circle the phonemic transcription that matches the pronunciation of the word you hear.

   1 /fæn/ _____ /fʌn/ _____

   2 /muːd/ _____ /mʌd/ _____

   3 /kuːl/ _____ /kɔːl/ _____

   4 /buːt/ _____ /bɔːt/ _____

   5 /fʊt/ _____ /fuːd/ _____

   6 /kʊd/ _____ /kɑːd/ _____

b) Write the words, with the correct spelling, in the spaces next to the phonemic transcriptions.

Task 2: Unstressed syllables: /ə/ and /ɪ/

Short /ə/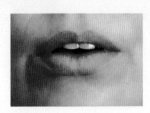

The mouth is relaxed and slightly open. The sound comes from the middle of the mouth.

The short /ə/ sound *only* appears in *unstressed* syllables. As can be seen from the examples given on the next page, there is no single written vowel form to represent /ə/. At the end of words, it may appear in written form as ~er, ~re, ~our, or ~or (as in *reader*, *meagre*, *favour* and *actor*). (Note: Many words ending with ~*our* in British English end with ~*or* in American English: fav*our*/fav*or*, flav*our*/flav*or*, harb*our*/harb*or*, etc.)

2.1 CD1 – 17 **Listen to these examples.**

> appear /əˈpɪə/   suggest /səˈdʒest/   effort /ˈefət/   colour /ˈkʌlə/

2.2 **Study the words 1–14 and do the following activities.**

a) Mark the stressed syllable with (').

b) Write /ə/ above any syllables that include this sound.

c) CD1 – 18 Listen and repeat the words.

Example: cŏmˈputĕr

1 affect
2 several
3 standard
4 failure
5 purpose
6 propose
7 author
8 attempt
9 distance
10 accept
11 opposite
12 flavour
13 compare
14 approach

Short /ɪ/

The tongue is quite close to the roof of the mouth and the lips are stretched. The sound comes from the front of the mouth.

In unstressed syllables where the vowel letter is written as e, it is often pronounced as a short /ɪ/.

2.3 CD1 – 19 **Listen to these examples.**

> describe /dɪsˈkraɪb/
>
> prefer /prɪˈfɜː/

2.4 **Study the words 1–7 and do the following activities.**

a) Mark the stressed syllable with (').

b) Write /ɪ/ above any syllables that include this sound.

c) CD1 – 20 Listen and repeat the words.

Example: rĕˈduce

1 invited

2 decision

3 demand

4 beyond

5 extensive

6 research

7 interpret

Task 3: Word stress patterns

Groups of nouns, adjectives and verbs with similar endings (or suffixes) often follow similar word stress patterns. In the groups of words below, the stress falls on the syllable *before* the ending (e.g., *~sion*, *~tion*, *~graphy*).

3.1 ⊙ **CD1 – 21 Listen and repeat the following words, making sure you stress the syllables in the columns highlighted in the tables below.**

Nouns ending in *~sion* or *~tion*

discussion
solution
occasion
definition
decision
position

dis	CUS	sion
so	LU	tion
oc	CA	sion
defi	NI	tion
de	CI	sion
po	SI	tion

Nouns ending in *~graphy*

geography
biography
photography

ge	O	graphy
bi	O	graphy
pho	TO	graphy

Adjectives ending in *~ic*

electric
economic
specific

e	LEC	tric
eco	NO	mic
spe	CI	fic

Nouns ending in *~ency* or *~ancy*

frequency
consultancy
consistency
vacancy
efficiency
redundancy

	FRE	quency
con	SUL	tancy
con	SIS	tency
	VA	cancy
ef	FI	ciency
re	DUN	dancy

Nouns ending in *~ium*

medium
uranium
consortium

	ME	dium
u	RA	nium
con	SOR	tium

Adjectives ending in ~ical

electrical
political
periodical

	e	LEC	trical
	po	LI	tical
	peri	O	dical

Nouns ending in ~ity

identity
authority
community

	i	DEN	tity
	au	THO	rity
	com	MU	nity

Adjectives ending in ~tial or ~cial

essential
financial
potential
commercial
residential
artificial

	es	ŞEN	tial
	fi	NAN	cial
	po	TEN	tial
	com	MER	cial
	resi	DEN	tial
	arti	FI	cial

Verbs ending in ~ify

modify
clarify
identify

		MO	dify
		CLA	rify
	i	DEN	tify

Nouns ending in ~logy

apology
technology
biology

	a	PO	logy
	tech	NO	logy
	bi	O	logy

Adjectives ending in ~tional

additional
international
optional

	a	DDI	tional
	inter	NA	tional
		OP	tional

3.2 **Study the words 1–12 and do the following activities.**

a) Mark the stressed syllable in each word, following the patterns in Ex 3.1.

b) 🎧 **CD1 – 22** Listen to check your answers. Repeat the words to practise your pronunciation.

1 academic

2 dimension

3 beneficial

4 similarity

5 majority

6 initial

7 demography

8 allergic

9 tradition

10 deficiency

11 conventional

12 justify

3.3 **Study the sentences below. Use words from Ex 3.1 to complete the sentences.**

a) Most of the course modules are compulsory, but there are two _____ modules.

b) The committee has not yet taken a _____ whether or not to award funding for the project.

c) It is important to start with a _____ of the term 'sustainable development', as it clearly means different things to different people.

d) Although solar power provides a _____ answer to some of the world's energy needs, at the moment the technology is quite expensive.

e) Have we really found a _____ to the problem?

f) It is hoped that the development of _____ intelligence will mean that computers will be able to think in the way humans do.

g) There is a lot of confusion, so it is essential to _____ the situation.

h) The stadium was built by an international _____ of construction companies.

i) There is a _____ for a laboratory technician, so the post will be advertized next week.

j) James Watson's _____ of Margaret Thatcher was published last month.

k) The organization plans to publish a new _____, with three issues a year.

l) Despite plans for _____ growth of five per cent over the next year, unemployment is continuing to rise.

m) We will need to _____ the design of the equipment after a number of weaknesses were discovered in the testing process.

n) Professor Jones is a leading _____ on 17th-century Italian literature.

o) The _____ areas of the new town will be located well away from the industrial and commercial zones.

🎧 **CD1 – 23 Now listen to check your answers.**

Practise your pronunciation by playing the recording again and pausing to repeat the sentences.

Task 4: Word families: Word stress and pronunciation

Word families are groups of words that have the same basic form and similar meanings. By adding prefixes or suffixes, you can generate nouns, adjectives, adverbs and verbs from the basic form. Learning word families is a useful technique for extending your range of vocabulary.

Word stress

In many cases, the word stress pattern does not change from one form of the word to another.

4.1 ⓦ **CD1 – 24 Listen to the following examples.**

Verb	Noun	Adjective
poss'ess	poss'ession	poss'essive
per'suade	per'suasion	per'suasive
ass'ess	ass'essment	ass'essed

However, in some cases the word stress may vary from one form to another. For example:

> 'analyze (v),   an'alysis (n),   ana'lytical (adj)

4.2 ⓦ **CD1 – 25 Listen and repeat these words. Mark the stressed syllable. The first one is done for you.**

Verb	Noun	Adjective
ap'ply	appli'cation	ap'plicable
activate	activity	active
inform	information	informative
–	probability	probable
socialize	society	social
experiment	experiment	experimental
equal	equality	equal
unite	union	united
transfer	transfer	transferable

You may also notice differences in the vowel or consonant sounds. For example, in *social* /ˈsəʊʃl/ and *society* /səˈsaɪəti:/, the first vowel sound is different in each word.

Even when the word stress does not change, there may be differences in pronunciation of the basic form.

4.3 ⓦ **CD1 – 26 Listen to these examples.**

occur (*v*)   /əˈkɜː/   occurrence (*n*) /əˈkʌrəns/

assume (*v*) /əˈsjuːm/   assumption (*n*) /əˈsʌmpʃən/

4.4 **Study the groups of sentences below and do activities a) and b).**

a) Complete the gaps with a form of the word printed in bold in the first sentence.

b) Mark the stressed syllable in the words that you write in the gaps.

Example:

We need to **'analyze** the data.
Statistical an'alysis of the data provided some unexpected results.
You need good ana'lytical skills for this kind of work.

1 The stomach **pro'duces** acids, which help to digest food.
The new model should be in _____ in November.
If the factory does not become more _____, it faces closure.
The _____ was withdrawn from sale after a number of defects were identified.

2 Four alternative **'methods** of payment are offered.
She takes a very _____ approach to her work.
They have been developing a new _____ for research in this area.

3 The president stated that **eco'nomic** development was the main priority.
The chancellor is concerned that the _____ is overheating.
She is studying _____ at Lancaster University.

4 Wages tend to be higher in the **'private** sector.
This law is intended to protect people's _____.
The water services industry was _____ in the 1980s.

5 The heights of plants **'varied** from 8 cm to 15 cm.
A wide _____ of fruit is grown on the island.
Regional _____ in the unemployment rate are significant.
A number of _____, such as wind speed and direction, humidity and air pressure, need to be considered.

6 Both approaches yielded **'similar** results.
There are many _____ between the two religions.
The firefighters resorted to industrial action to settle the dispute. _____, railway workers are threatening to strike because of changes in working practices.

4.5 ⊙ **CD1 – 27 Listen to the sentences and correct any that you got wrong.**

In this unit, you have learnt six English vowel sounds: /ɒ/, /ʌ/, /ə/, /ʊ/, /ɔː/, /uː/, and practised their pronunciation. You have also become more aware of weak forms and looked at different word stress patterns.

1  **CD1 – 28 Listen to the words in the box. Then match them to the phonemic transcriptions below.**

| other | ankle | pull | shot | uncle | pool | short | another |

a) /ənʌðə/

b) /puːl/

c) /ʃɔːt/

d) /pʊl/

e) /ʌŋkəl/

f) /æŋkəl/

g) /ʌðə/

h) /ʃɒt/

2 **Choose seven multi-syllable nouns that are connected with your field of study. (If you like, you can include words that you have already studied in this unit.) For each word, do the following:**

a) Write the word and mark the syllable that is stressed.

b) Check the pronunciation of the word in a learner's dictionary. Do you pronounce the unstressed syllable(s) using the sounds /ə/ or /ɪ/?

c) Does the word belong to a word family? Write as many other related words as you can think of, e.g., verb and adjective forms or other nouns with the same root.

For web resources, see:

www.englishforacademicstudy.com/student/pronunciation/links

These weblinks will provide you with further practice in areas of pronunciation such as the sounds, stress and intonation patterns of English.

3

Consonant sounds 1, sentence stress

In this unit you will:
- learn about the pronunciation of voiced and unvoiced consonants;
- practise recognizing and producing these sounds;
- learn to identify stressed words in sentences;
- practise using sentence stress to highlight important information.

Task 1: Voiced and unvoiced consonants

There are a number of pairs of consonants that are pronounced in the same way, except that one consonant is *unvoiced* and the other is *voiced*.

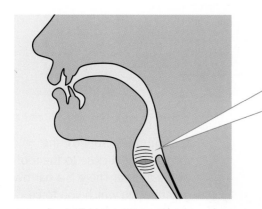

For **voiced** consonants /b/, /d/, /g/, etc., the vocal chords in your throat vibrate.

For **unvoiced** consonants /p/, /t/, /k/, etc., there is *no* vibration.

1.1   🎧 **CD1 – 29 Listen and repeat these continuous sounds.**

SSSSSSSSSSSSSSSSS

ZZZZZZZZZZZZZZZZZ

The position of your tongue, lips and mouth is more or less the same for each sound, but for the /z/ sound there is also vibration of your vocal chords, so we say that /z/ is a *voiced* consonant. There is no vibration for the /s/ sound, so it is *unvoiced*.

/s/ is **unvoiced**, e.g., snow

/z/ is **voiced**, e.g., zero

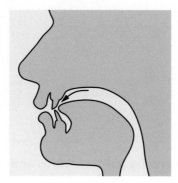

For both these sounds, the tip of the tongue is held close to the part of the mouth just above the teeth. There is a narrow gap through which you force air.

In the table on page 24, each pair of consonants (/p/ and /b/, /t/ and /d/, etc.) is pronounced in the same way, except that one is voiced and the other is unvoiced.

1.2 🎧 CD1 – 30 **Listen and repeat each pair of words. Can you hear the difference in pronunciation?**

Unvoiced		Voiced	
/p/	pie	/b/	buy
/t/	town	/d/	down
/k/	coal	/g/	goal
/s/	sink	/z/	zinc
/ʃ/	mesh	/ʒ/	measure
/tʃ/	chunk	/dʒ/	junk
/f/	fast	/v/	vast
/θ/	breath	/ð/	breathe

/ʃ/ is **unvoiced**, e.g., mesh

/ʒ/ is **voiced**, e.g., measure

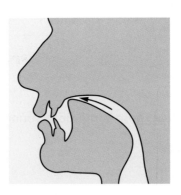

For both these sounds, the tongue is held close to the roof of the mouth. There is a narrow gap through which you force air. Compare these sounds with /s/ and /z/ on page 23. You will see the tongue is higher and further back in the mouth.

/f/ is **unvoiced**, e.g., fast

/v/ is **voiced**, e.g., vast

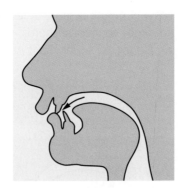

For both these sounds, the inside part of the bottom lip is held against the top teeth. Pressure is released as you bring the bottom lip away from the top teeth.

1.3 🎧 CD1 – 31 **Look at the following pairs of words and circle the word you hear.**

Each pair is pronounced in the same way, except that one consonant is unvoiced and the other is voiced.

Example: pill (bill)

	Unvoiced	Voiced
a)	paste	based
b)	simple	symbol
c)	tense	dense
d)	try	dry
e)	white	wide
f)	card	guard
g)	class	glass
h)	ankle	angle
i)	sown	zone
j)	price	prize
k)	use (*n*)	use (*v*)
l)	advice (*n*)	advise (*v*)
m)	rich	ridge
n)	batch	badge
o)	few	view
p)	proof (*n*)	prove (*v*)
q)	belief (*n*)	believe (*v*)

Check your answers on page 95. Then listen and repeat the words with the correct voiced or unvoiced consonant.

1.4 🎧 CD1 – 32 **Listen and complete these sentences or phrases.**

a) **1** a ＿＿＿＿＿ situation ＿＿
   2 a ＿＿＿＿＿ material ＿＿

b) **1** a ＿＿＿＿＿ area ＿＿
   2 as ＿＿＿＿＿ as a sheet ＿＿

c) **1** at the ＿＿＿＿＿ of the plant ＿＿
   2 the ＿＿＿＿＿ of change ＿＿

d) **1** Public ＿＿＿＿＿ have improved. ＿＿
   2 A cube has six ＿＿＿＿＿. ＿＿

e) **1** difficult to ＿＿＿＿＿ ＿＿
   2 It's had good ＿＿＿＿＿. ＿＿

f) **1** the ＿＿＿＿＿ of the fire ＿＿
   2 It changed the ＿＿＿＿＿ of his life. ＿＿

1.5 **Write *U* or *V* beside each sentence or phrase to show if the missing word has an unvoiced or a voiced consonant.**

Example: a <u>tense</u> situation <u>U</u>

1.6 **Listen again and repeat the sentences or phrases, focusing on accurate pronunciation.**

Task 2: /θ/, /t/ and /s/

2.1 @ **CD1 – 33 Listen to the difference in pronunciation between these pairs of words.**

/θ/	/s/
thing	sing
path	pass
worth	worse
mouth	mouse
youth	use

/θ/	/t/
thin	tin
thank	tank
thread	tread
both	boat
death	debt

Listen again and repeat the words.

Pronunciation note

/θ/ is always written as *th* (*think, both*).

2.2 @ **CD1 – 34 You will hear some of the words from Ex 2.1. Circle the phonemic transcription that matches the pronunciation of the word you hear.**

Example: /θɪn/   /tɪn/

a)	/θænk/	/tænk/
b)	/deθ/	/det/
c)	/bəʊθ/	/bəʊt/
d)	/wɜːθ/	/wɜːs/
e)	/pɑːθ/	/pɑːs/
f)	/maʊθ/	/maʊs/
g)	/ʃuːθ/	/ʃuːs/

2.3 **Complete these sentences with words from Ex 2.1.**

a) The painting is supposed to be _____ £5 million.

b) The fuel is stored in a 30-litre _____.

c) Cancer is the leading cause of _____ among women.

d) A _____ layer of plastic is needed to provide waterproofing.

e) I couldn't follow the _____ of his argument.

f) The _____ is, no one likes to be criticized.

g) Tax increases are necessary to finance the national _____.

2.4 @ **CD1 – 35 Now listen to the correct answers and repeat the sentences.**

Task 3: /ð/

/ð/ occurs as the first sound in a number of common function words.

3.1 🎧 **CD1 – 36 Listen and repeat these words.**

the	this	these	that	those	they	their*
	there*	theirs	than	then	though	

* These words have the same pronunciation.

Pronunciation note

/ð/ is always written as *th* (*this, other*).

This sound also occurs at the end of some common words as /ðə/, spelt ~*ther*.

weather**	whether**	gather	either	neither	together	bother	rather
	other	another	further	mother	father	brother	

** These words have the same pronunciation.

3.2 🎧 **CD1 – 37 Listen to these sentences and phrases and repeat them.**

a) What's the weather like there?

b) Let's get together.

c) I'd rather not.

d) I wouldn't bother.

e) I don't like them.

f) I don't like them, either.

g) … further down the road …

h) … the other day …

Task 4: /θ/ and /ð/

/θ/ is **unvoiced**, e.g., <u>th</u>in

/ð/ is **voiced**, e.g., <u>th</u>e

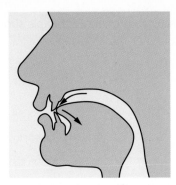

For both these sounds, the tip of the tongue is held against the back of the teeth. Pressure is released as you bring the tip of the tongue away from the teeth.

4.1 🎧 CD1 – 38 **Listen to these two words.**

thank	/θæŋk/
than	/ðæn/

To pronounce both /θ/ and /ð/, you put the tip of your tongue against the back of your teeth, but /ð/ is also *voiced*. Can you hear how /ð/ has a heavier sound than /θ/?

4.2 🎧 CD1 – 39 **Listen to these phrases and write in the correct symbols above the words.**

                     ð   θ
Example: … another thing to consider is …

a) … in theory …

b) … the truth is that …

c) … the growth rate …

d) … a further theme …

e) … they thought that ….

f) … this method …

g) … beneath the surface …

h) … this therapy might be used to …

i) … youth culture …

Now listen again and repeat the phrases.

Pronunciation note

If you find the /θ/ sound difficult to pronounce, people should still understand from the context if you replace it with the /s/ sound or the /t/ sound.

So, if you can't say …	try saying …
thank	*sank, tank*
thin	*sin, tin*
worth	*worse*

Similarly, if you find the /ð/ sound difficult to pronounce, people should still understand from the context if you replace it with the /z/ sound or the /d/ sound.

So, if you can't say …	try saying …
they	*day*
then	*zen, den*
breathe	*breeze*

Task 5: Sentence stress

While word stress (or accent) is generally decided by language rules, sentence stress (or prominence) is decided by speaker choice. The speaker usually chooses to stress content words, which carry the information, and not structure or function words, such as auxiliary verbs, pronouns, prepositions and determiners, although this is not always the case.

5.1 🎧 **CD1 – 40 Listen to this recording of the previous paragraph.**

You will hear that the underlined words sound stronger than the other words. These are the words that the speaker has chosen to stress.

While <u>word</u> stress (or <u>accent</u>) is generally decided by language <u>rules</u>, <u>sentence</u> stress (or <u>prominence</u>) is decided by <u>speaker</u> <u>choice</u>. The <u>speaker</u> usually chooses to stress <u>content</u> words, which carry the <u>information</u>, and not <u>structure</u> or <u>function</u> words, such as <u>auxiliary</u> verbs, <u>pronouns</u>, <u>prepositions</u> and <u>determiners</u>, although this is not <u>always</u> the case.

5.2 🎧 **CD1 – 41 Listen to these sentences, in which the sentence stress changes according to the meaning.**

You **have** to hand in the essay on Monday   … there's a **strict deadline**.

You have to hand in the **essay** on Monday   … not the **report**.

You have to hand in the essay on **Monday**   … not **Wednesday**.

Practise repeating them with the correct sentence stress.

5.3 🎧 **CD1 – 42 Listen to these beginnings of sentences and choose the more suitable ending, according to the sentence stress.**

a) Well, we know how this happened, …

☐ … but do other people know?

☐ … but do we know why it happened?

b) Having looked at the effect of deforestation on the environment, …

☐ … we will now discuss greenhouse gases and the roles they play.

☐ … we will now consider its effect on the economy.

c) Most of our cotton is imported, …

☐ … but we produce about 500,000 tonnes a year.

☐ … but we are self-sufficient in wool.

d) The crime rate fell by 15 per cent last year, …

☐ … but this year it's risen.

☐ … but this year the figure is nearer to 8 per cent.

e) The oil pump needs replacing, ...

☐ ... not the filter.

☐ ... as it can't be repaired.

5.4 🎧 **CD1 – 43 Now listen to the complete sentences to check your answers.**

Can you hear how words are contrasted through stress in different parts of each sentence?

5.5 🎧 **CD1 – 44 Read and listen to an extract from a lecture called *Introduction to British Agriculture*. Underline the words you hear stressed.**

> As a backdrop to all of these activities, particularly after the Second World War, a lot of effort was put into research and development of agriculture in terms of plant breeding, breeding crops that were higher yielding, that were perhaps disease-resistant, and so on and so forth. Also, crops that might have better quality, better bread-making quality, higher gluten content, to make them doughy, higher protein content, and so on and so forth. Research, too, and this is again at one of the university farms, research into livestock production. Understanding how to better manage our livestock, again to make them produce more, certainly, but also to produce and influence the quality of the livestock products, whether that happens to be milk or cheese, come back to that in a moment, or indeed meat.

5.6 **Why do you think the speaker chose to stress those words? Listen to the extract again and repeat it sentence by sentence.**

5.7 🎧 **CD1 – 45 Read and listen to part of a lecture on globalization. Underline the words you hear stressed.**

> Now to get to the meat of the lecture, the basic purpose of this lecture is to give you some overview of the kind of contemporary academic and policy debate about globalization and particularly about a very specific, although rather general, debate itself, that is the debate on the effect of globalization on the role of the state. So, you see on the overhead, the lecture's going to be kind of in two parts: the first will be looking at globalization, causes and consequences, and more particularly a kind of definition of the discussion of some of the competing conceptions of globalization, that is, you know, what people say it is, so that we can then discuss in some detail, hopefully, this question of how globalization's affecting the state.

5.8 **Why do you think the speaker chose to stress those words? Listen to the extract again and repeat it sentence by sentence.**

Unit Summary

In this unit, you have learnt about voiced and unvoiced consonant sounds, practised distinguishing between commonly confused sounds and focused on pronouncing the sounds /θ/and /ð/. You have also become more aware of sentence stress and how it is used to highlight information.

1 **Study the words in the box and say them aloud.**

lose	proof	surge	three	very	seem	free	theme
	loose	ferry	prove		search		

a) Which words have a similar pronunciation and could be confused?

b) Can you think of any other English words that are easily confused with each other?

2 **Practise saying the sentences by stressing the underlined words.**

a) You can take notes <u>during</u> the lecture or <u>after</u> it.

You <u>can</u> take notes during the lecture, but you don't <u>have</u> to.

<u>You</u> can take notes during the lecture, but <u>I'm</u> not going to!

b) <u>Exports</u> rose by three per cent last year, but <u>imports</u> fell.

Exports <u>rose</u> by three per cent last year, after years of <u>decline</u>.

Exports rose by <u>three</u> per cent last year, not the <u>eight</u> per cent reported in the media.

3 **In each sentence, underline two words that you would expect to be stressed to contrast information. Practise saying the sentences with these words stressed.**

a) Some species of shark attack people, but most are harmless.

b) There used to be a Chemistry Department, but it closed in 2006.

c) The aid provided to the victims was too little, too late.

d) Many banks stopped lending, when the government wanted them to lend more.

🎧 **CD1 – 46 Listen and compare your ideas with the recording.**

4 **Think about what you have studied in this unit and answer the questions below.**

a) Which exercises did you find most challenging?

b) Which consonant sounds do you confuse or find difficult to pronounce?

c) How is it helpful to study the phonemic symbols for different sounds?

d) Why is it helpful to be more aware of stressed words in a sentence?

For web resources, see:

www.englishforacademicstudy.com/student/pronunciation/links

These weblinks will provide you with further practice in areas of pronunciation such as the sounds, stress and intonation patterns of English.

Consonant sounds 2, word stress on two-syllable words

In this unit you will:
- learn more phonemic symbols representing consonant sounds;
- practise recognizing and producing these consonant sounds;
- learn where to place the stress in words with two syllables.

Consonant sounds

In this unit, you will focus on the consonants shaded in this table.

/p/	/t/	/k/	/s/	/ʃ/	/tʃ/	/f/	/θ/
post	take	keep	snow	shoe	choice	leaf	thin
/b/	/d/	/g/	/z/	/ʒ/	/dʒ/	/v/	/ð/
book	doctor	goal	zero	measure	jump	leave	the
/h/	/m/	/n/	/ŋ/	/l/	/r/	/w/	/j/
hotel	meet	nine	bring	late	red	well	yes

Task 1: /ʒ/

Words ending in *~sion* are sometimes pronounced /~ʒən/ and sometimes /~ʃən/.

1.1 🎧 **CD1 – 47 Listen to the pronunciation of the words in the box and write them under the correct heading.**

| decision version dimension occasion conclusion discussion expression |
| admission expansion supervision confusion erosion |

/~ʒən/	/~ʃən/

Before checking your answers, try and see a pattern in the spelling that helps you decide how *~sion* is pronounced.

Words ending in ~*sure* are sometimes pronounced /~ʒə/, sometimes /~ʃə/ and sometimes /ʃɔː/.

1.2 🔊 **CD1 – 48 Listen to the three different pronunciations of the word endings in the box and write them under the correct heading.**

| measure | pressure | closure | assure | ensure | pleasure | leisure | exposure |

/~ʒə/	/~ʃə/	/ʃɔː/

Note: The pattern in spelling for words ending in ~*sure* is similar to that of Ex 1.1.

Words which include the letters ~*sual* also usually follow the pattern in Exs 1.1 and 1.2.

1.3 🔊 **CD1 – 49 Listen and repeat the following words.**

| visual | casual | usually | sensual |

Task 2: /v/

2.1 🔊 **CD1 – 50 Listen to and repeat the following words and phrases.**

| visit | develop | value | average | village | very good service |
| violent | every level | voice | When does it arrive? |

2.2 **Listen and repeat again, this time recording your pronunciation. Play back the recording and evaluate your pronunciation. How accurate is it?**

Pronunciation note

If you find the /v/ sound difficult to pronounce, people should still understand if you replace it with the /f/ sound (but not the /w/ sound).

So, if you can't say …   try saying …

vast	*fast*
view	*few*
invest	*infest*
service	*surface*

2.3 **If you had problems pronouncing /v/, do Ex 2.1 again, replacing /v/ with /f/.**

Task 3: /j/

3.1 CD1 – 51 **The /j/ sound appears at the beginning of words starting with _y~_.**
Listen and repeat.

> yet   young   yellow   year   yesterday

3.2 CD1 – 52 **The /j/ sound also appears at the beginning of some words starting with _u~_. Tick (✓) the words below that are pronounced /juː~/.**

a) ☐ union

b) ☐ unless

c) ☐ uniform

d) ☐ uncle

e) ☐ unclear

f) ☐ unusual

g) ☐ useful

h) ☐ username

i) ☐ usual

j) ☐ uranium

k) ☐ until

l) ☐ urgent

Check your answers, listen and repeat the words.

Note: The negative forms of adjectives (e.g., _unimportant_, _unlikely_) are pronounced /ʌn~/.

3.3 CD1 – 53 **You also find the /j/ sound in the middle of words, represented by _y_. Listen to these examples.**

> beyond   layer   layout   buyer

3.4 CD1 – 54 **Sometimes, the /j/ sound in the middle of words is not represented by any character. Listen to these words and mark the position of the /j/ sound in them.**

Examples: n/j/ew   contin/j/ue   comp/j/uter

a) fuel

b) view

c) argue

d) education

e) cube

f) few

g) rescue

h) distribute

i) assume

Listen again and repeat the words.

Task 4: /ʃ/ and /tʃ/

4.1 ⊙ CD1 – 55 **Listen to the difference in pronunciation between these pairs of words.**

/ʃ/	/tʃ/
ship	chip
shop	chop
share	chair
shoes	choose
cash	catch
washed	watched
dishes	ditches

Listen again and repeat the words.

Pronunciation note

/ʃ/ is usually written as *sh* (*show, wash*).
/tʃ/ is usually written as *ch* (*cheap, rich*) or as *tch* (*watch*).

4.2 ⊙ CD1 – 56 **You will hear some of the words from Ex 4.1. Circle the phonemic transcription that matches the pronunciation of the word you hear.**

Example: /ʃɒp/ (/tʃɒp/)

a) /kæʃ/ /kætʃ/

b) /ʃuːz/ /tʃuːz/

c) /wɒʃd/ /wɒtʃt/

d) /ʃeə/ /tʃeə/

e) /dɪʃɪz/ /dɪtʃɪz/

f) /ʃɪp/ /tʃɪp/

4.3 Complete these sentences with words from Ex 4.1.

a) There's a small _____ on the card which stores your personal data.

b) You can pay with _____ or by cheque.

c) Farmers need to dig _____ to drain the soil.

d) The _____ value has shot up by 30 per cent!

e) You can _____ which topic to write about for your assignment.

f) The sample should be _____ in a five per cent saline solution before analysis.

4.4 ⊙ CD1 – 57 **Listen to the correct answers and repeat the sentences.**

Task 5: /tʃ/ and /dʒ/

/tʃ/ is **unvoiced**, e.g., <u>ch</u>oice

/dʒ/ is **voiced**, e.g., <u>j</u>ump

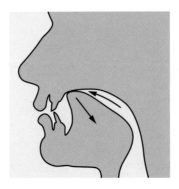

For both these sounds, the flat part of the tongue is held against the roof of the mouth. Pressure is released as you bring the tongue away from the roof of the mouth.

5.1 ⊙ CD1 – 58 **Listen to the difference in pronunciation between these pairs of words.**

/tʃ/	/dʒ/
chunk	junk
cheap	Jeep
H	age
search	surge
rich	ridge
batch	badge

Listen again and repeat the words.

> ## Pronunciation note
>
> /dʒ/ is sometimes written as *j* (*join*, *jump*) and sometimes as *g* (*general*, *imagine*).
>
> **Note:** *g* is also often pronounced /g/ (*begin*, *girl*, *give*).

5.2 ⊙ CD1 – 59 **You will hear some of the words from Ex 5.1. Circle the phonemic transcription that matches the pronunciation of the word you hear.**

Example: (/sɜːtʃ/)   /sɜːdʒ/

a)   /rɪtʃ/   /rɪdʒ/
b)   /eɪdʒ/   /eɪtʃ/
c)   /tʃʌnk/   /dʒʌnk/
d)   /bætʃ/   /bædʒ/
e)   /tʃiːp/   /dʒiːp/

5.3 **Complete these sentences with words from Ex 5.1.**

    a) Most fruit and vegetables are _____ in vitamins.

    b) Credit card bills are generally prepared by _____ processing of data.

    c) A large _____ of the budget is spent on overheads.

    d) There is a _____ of high pressure running from north-west to south-east.

    e) Children today eat too much _____ food.

    f) A sudden _____ in the power supply can damage your computer.

5.4 CD1 – 60 **Listen to the correct answers and repeat the sentences.**

Task 6: Word stress on two-syllable words

6.1 CD1 – 61 **Put the words into the correct column, according to their stress pattern.**

provide   system   assist   reason   prepare   appear
recent   receive   include   certain   factor   question
problem   modern   suggest   reduce   private   observe

Example:

Oo	oO
question	provide

6.2 CD1 – 62 **Listen to these pairs of sentences and underline the syllable that is stressed in the words in bold.**

Example:

Coffee is this country's biggest '**export**.
They **ex'port** coffee mainly to Europe.

    a) There has been a significant **increase** in unemployment.
        It has been decided to **increase** the interest rate by a quarter of a per cent.

b) You need to keep a **record** of all the references you use in the essay.
She wants to **record** the lecture with her MP3 player.

c) About 30 people were **present** at the seminar.
He plans to **present** the results of his research at the conference.

Now study the answers to Exs 6.1 and 6.2. Can you see a pattern in the pronunciation?

6.3 **Complete the explanation of the 'rules' for word stress in two-syllable words, using the words in the box.**

nouns   verbs   adjectives

Most two-syllable _____ and _____ have stress on the first syllable.

Most two-syllable _____ have stress on the second syllable.

6.4 **CD1 – 63 Unlike the two-syllable words in Ex 6.3, the stress in words ending in ~er, ~ry, ~le, ~ion, ~age, ~ish, ~ow and ~us generally falls on the first syllable. Listen and repeat these words.**

~er	~ry	~le	~ion
answer	angry	angle	action
gather	hurry	handle	mention
matter	story	middle	nation
suffer	vary	trouble	question
~age	**~ish**	**~ow**	**~us**
damage	English	follow	
language	finish	narrow	focus
manage	publish	shadow	minus
package	rubbish	window	

Note: The words *prefer*, *refer* and *allow* are some exceptions to this rule: they all have stress on the second syllable.

Unit Summary

In this unit, you have learnt six English consonant sounds: /ʃ/, /tʃ/, /ʒ/, /dʒ/, /v/, /j/, and practised their pronunciation. You have also become more aware of where to place the stress on words with two syllables.

1   **Each of the words in the box contains one of the consonant sounds in the table. Write them in the correct column below.**

> confusion   choices   unusual   average
> distribution   innovation   watched   suggest

/ʃ/	/tʃ/	/dʒ/	/z/

2   **Practise saying the words from Ex 1 and decide which words also contain other consonant sounds that you have studied in this unit (/v/ and /j/).**

3   🔊 **CD1 – 64 Listen to the following pairs of sentences, which contain words in bold with the same spelling. Mark the stressed syllable in each pair of words. For which pairs is the word stress the same, and for which is it different?**

a) The **contracts** were signed last week.
     The metal **contracts** as it cools down.

b) It caused a lot of **damage**.
     How does it **damage** your health?

c) Why did they **object** to the proposal?
     Archaeologists are not sure what this **object** was used for.

d) What is the main **focus** of your research?
     We need to **focus** on the real issues.

> For web resources, see:
> **www.englishforacademicstudy.com/student/pronunciation/links**
> These weblinks will provide you with further practice in areas of pronunciation such as the sounds, stress and intonation patterns of English.

5 Diphthongs 1, sounds in connected speech

In this unit you will:
- learn which phonemic symbols represent certain diphthongs;
- practise recognizing and producing diphthongs;
- learn how the pronunciation of words is affected by their context in connected speech.

Diphthongs

Diphthongs can be thought of as combinations of two vowels. For example, the /eɪ/ sound in *day* starts as /e/ and then ends /ɪ/.

In this unit, you will focus on the diphthongs shaded in this table.

/aɪ/	/aʊ/	/əʊ/	/eɪ/	/eə/	/ɪə/	/ɔɪ/	/ʊə/
wh<u>y</u>	n<u>ow</u>	g<u>o</u>	d<u>ay</u>	c<u>are</u>	d<u>ear</u>	enj<u>oy</u>	p<u>ure</u>

Task 1: /aɪ/ and /ɪ/

1.1　　◉ CD2 – 1 **Put the words in the box into the correct column, according to the pronunciation of the vowel or diphthong sound.**

> time　think　life　write　while　win　high
> try　sit　site　buy　bit　might　sign　like

/aɪ/	/ɪ/

Pronunciation note

(**C** = consonant)

The /aɪ/ sound often occurs in:

- one-syllable words ending ~i**C**e: *fine, rise, drive;*
- words including **C**igh: *light, fight, thigh;*
- one-syllable words written **CC**y: *why, sky, dry.*

The /ɪ/ sound:

- is often written **C**i**C**: *lid, fit, ship;*
- often occurs in unstressed syllables: *decíde, mínute (n).*

However, there are exceptions to these patterns, e.g., *give, live (v).*

1.2 **Check how your answers to Ex 1.1 fit these patterns.**

1.3 🔊 **CD2 – 2 How do you pronounce *L-I-V-E* in each of these sentences?**

   a) Where do you live?

   b) The match is being shown live on TV.

   Why is the pronunciation different in each sentence?

1.4 🔊 **CD2 – 3 Listen to the six words below and complete the two activities.**

   a) Circle the phonemic transcription that matches the pronunciation of the word you hear.

   1 /wɪl/ _____   /waɪl/ _____

   2 /fɪt/ _____   /faɪt/ _____

   3 /stɪl/ _____   /staɪl/ _____

   4 /hɪt/ _____   /haɪt/ _____

   5 /lɪtə/ _____   /laɪtə/ _____

   6 /hɪd/ _____   /haɪd/ _____

   b) Now write the words, with the correct spelling, in the spaces next to the phonemic transcriptions.

1.5 🔊 **CD2 – 4 Underline the /aɪ/ sounds in these sentences or phrases. Then listen and repeat them.**

   a) Try the other side.

   b) The height's fine.

   c) This type of plant needs a lot of light.

   d) There was a slight rise in the share value.

Task 2: /əʊ/ and /ɒ/

2.1 🎧 **CD2 – 5 Put the words in the box into the correct column, according to the pronunciation of the vowel or diphthong sound.**

cost	coast	show	rod	road	grow	lot	load
	flow	hope	code	cold	not	note	fold

/əʊ/	/ɒ/

Pronunciation note

(**C** = consonant)

The /əʊ/ sound often occurs in:

- one-syllable words ending ~o**C**e: *drove, hole, tone;*
- words including *oa*: *loan, float, coat;*
- words ending ~*ow*: *throw, slow, below.*

The /ɒ/ sound:

- is often written **C**o**C**: *got, sock, shop;*
- is sometimes written *a*: *what, wash, want.*

However, there are exceptions to these patterns.

- *more, some, gone*
- *board, abroad, coarse*
- *now, how*

2.2 **Check how your answers to Ex 2.1 fit these patterns.**

2.3 🎧 **CD2 – 6 Listen to the six words below and complete the activities.**

a) Listen and circle the phonemic transcription that matches the pronunciation of the word you hear.

1 /kɒst/ _____ /kəʊst/ _____

2 /nɒt/ _____ /nəʊt/ _____

3 /rɒd/ _____ /rəʊd/ _____

4 /sɒk/ _____ /səʊk/ _____

5 /wɒnt/ _____ /wəʊnt/ _____

6 /fɒnd/ _____ /fəʊnd/ _____

b) Write the words, with the correct spelling, in the spaces next to the phonemic transcriptions.

2.4 🎧 **CD2 – 7 Underline the /əʊ/ sounds in these sentences or phrases. Then listen and repeat.**

a) Most of the gold is exported.

b) … the hole in the ozone layer …

c) Gross profits were down.

d) Can you cope with the workload?

Task 3: /eɪ/, /æ/ and /ɑː/

3.1 🎧 **CD2 – 8 Put the words in the box into the correct column, according to the pronunciation of the vowel or diphthong sound.**

| plan   plane   dark   face   make   scale   large   lack |
| heart   play   weigh   gain   part   claim   bad |

/eɪ/	/æ/	/ɑː/

Pronunciation note

(**C** = consonant)

The /eɪ/ sound often occurs in:

- one-syllable words ending ~a**C**e: *place, rate, save*;
- words ending ~ay: *away, stay, today*;
- one-syllable words with *ai*: *paint, raise, train*.

The /ɑː/ sound is often written *ar*, but the *r* is often silent in British English: *far, start, hard*.

However, there are exceptions to these patterns, e.g., *have, care*.

3.2   **Check how your answers to Ex 3.1 fit these patterns.**

3.3   🎧 **CD2 – 9 Listen to the eight words below and complete the activities.**

a) Circle the phonemic transcription that matches the pronunciation of the word you hear.

1	/læk/	/leɪk/	
2	/tæp/	/teɪp/	
3	/plæn/	/pleɪn/	
4	/lætə/	/leɪtə/	
5	/ɑːm/	/eɪm/	
6	/mɑːk/	/meɪk/	
7	/pɑːs/	/peɪs/	
8	/kɑːm/	/keɪm/	

b) Now write the words, with the correct spelling, in the spaces next to the phonemic transcriptions.

3.4   🎧 **CD2 – 10 Underline the /eɪ/ sounds in these sentences or phrases. Then listen and repeat.**

a) Can you explain this heavy rainfall?

b) That's quite a claim to make.

c) The future remains uncertain.

d) The failure rate is quite high.

Task 4: Sounds in connected speech

4.1 🎧 **CD2 – 11 Listen to these short conversations.**

a) What do we need to solve the problem? A system.

b) What would you like me to do? Assist him.

In the two conversations, each response sounds almost identical. When you are talking, the pronunciation of some words is affected by the words before or after them.

● Words may seem to be *joined* together (linking).

● A sound may be *inserted* between words.

● A sound may *disappear* or be very difficult to hear.

● A sound may *change*.

Linking: Consonant + vowel

4.2 🎧 **CD2 – 12 Listen to the following examples.**

hand‿in

split‿up

complex‿issue

When a word ends in a consonant sound and the next word begins with a vowel sound, the words may seem to be linked.

4.3 🎧 **CD2 – 13 Listen to these phrases and repeat them, linking the words together where this is indicated.**

a) divide‿in two

b) historical‿evidence

c) as soon‿as possible

d) take‿over control

e) it'll‿end next week

f) the Data Protection‿Act

g) a wide‿area

h) keep‿up with‿it

i) an‿increase‿in crime

j) the main‿aim

4.4 🎧 **CD2 – 14 Listen to this introduction from a talk about home ownership and write in the links between words.**

> In this presentation I'm going to talk about home ownership in the UK. First I'm going to focus on changes in the patterns of home ownership in the last 20 years and provide an explanation for these changes. Then I'm going to describe the process of buying or selling a house. Finally I'm going to try to make some predictions about the housing market.

4.5 **Listen again and repeat the text in sections. Try to link words where this is appropriate.**

Inserting sounds between words: Vowel (V) + vowel

4.6 🎧 **CD2 – 15 Listen to the following examples.**

…V/w/V…

slow/w/economic growth

true/w/identity

go/w/up

Where a word ends with a vowel and the next word starts with a vowel, it is often easier to pronounce if we insert /w/, /ʝ/ or /ɾ/ between the vowels.

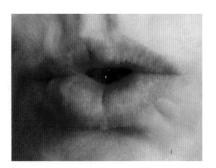

If the first word ends in a vowel pronounced with *rounded lips*, we often insert a /w/ sound. In the written form, the first word may end in *w*.

Listen again and see if you can produce the /w/ sound.

4.7 🎧 **CD2 – 16 Listen to the following examples.**

…V/ʝ/V…

carry/ʝ/on

high/ʝ/altitude

free/ʝ/access

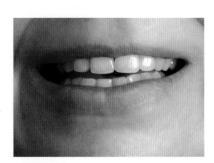

If the first word ends in a vowel pronounced with *stretched lips*, we often insert a /ʝ/ sound. In the written form, the first word may end in *y*.

Listen again and see if you can produce the /ʝ/ sound.

4.8 CD2 – 17 **Listen to the following examples.**

...V/ɾ/V...

aware/ɾ/of the problem

after/ɾ/all

faster/ɾ/access

If the first word ends in the /ə/ sound, we often insert the /r/ sound. In the written form, the first word may end in ~re, ~er or ~or.

Listen again and see if you can produce the /r/ sound.

Note: Most speakers of British English do not pronounce the *r* at the ends of words unless the word is followed by a vowel. However, many speakers of other Englishes, for example American English, *do* pronounce the *r* in most contexts.

4.9 CD2 – 18 **Listen to these phrases and decide if a /w/, /j/ or /ɾ/ sound needs to be inserted.**

a) try out

b) agree on this

c) two of them

d) driver error

e) radio operator

f) media event

g) high above the Earth

h) How does this tie in?

4.10 **Listen again and repeat the phrases, inserting the sounds where appropriate.**

In this unit, you have learnt the phonemic symbols for the diphthongs /aɪ/, /əʊ/ and /eɪ/ and looked at sound/spelling patterns for words that contain them. You have also become more aware of how the pronunciation of words is affected by their context in connected speech.

1   🎧 **CD2 – 19 Underline the diphthong sounds /aɪ/ in sentence (a), /əʊ/ in sentence (b) and /eɪ/ in sentence (c).**

a)   I think I'd like to carry on with Life Sciences, but I'm also interested in Psychology.

b)   I want to go into social work, so I'm studying Sociology.

c)   He came to Cardiff to give a paper on International Relations.

2   **Identify the words in the sentences in Ex 1 that would normally be linked. Draw in the links like this:**

I‿think‿I'd like to‿carry …

Listen again and check your answers.

3   **Study the words below; they are all from the sentences in Ex 1. Which sounds are normally inserted between them to make them easier to pronounce in connected speech?**

a)   carry on

b)   go into

c)   paper on

4   **Practise saying the sentences aloud, using the connected speech features you have looked at in the unit.**

5   **Think about the statements below. Do you agree or disagree with them?**

a)   It is more important to be able to hear the difference between English vowel sounds and diphthongs than to be able to produce them all correctly.

b)   Learners need to be able to understand how English speakers link sounds and words together, but don't need to speak in the same way themselves.

For web resources, see:

www.englishforacademicstudy.com/student/pronunciation/links

These weblinks will provide you with further practice in areas of pronunciation such as the sounds, stress and intonation patterns of English.

6 Consonant clusters 1, tone units 1

In this unit you will:
- learn how to pronounce groups of consonants (consonant clusters) at the beginning and in the middle of words;
- learn how to divide up connected speech into tone units.

Consonant clusters

In English, you may find groups of two or three consonant sounds:

- at the beginning of words: *grow, square, straight*;
- in the middle of words: *computer, expression, congratulate*;
- at the end of words: *hoped, branch, strength*;
- across two words: *room number, clamp down.*

In other languages, there may be a tendency for the pattern to be consonant – vowel – consonant – vowel, and speakers of such languages may find it difficult to pronounce certain consonant clusters.

Task 1: Consonant clusters at the beginning of words

1.1   ⦿ **CD2 – 20 Listen and repeat these groups of words, which begin with consonant clusters.**

blame blind blood	platform plenty plus	claim climate closure	glass global glue	flexible flight flow
brand break brief	practice pressure profit	create crucial criteria	graphics ground growth	fraction freeze frequent
draw draft drop	transaction trend trigger	quarter quality quota	twelve twice twin	threat through throw
				shrink shred

Note which of these consonant clusters you have problems pronouncing and try to focus on these in future practice.

1.2   ⦿ **CD2 – 21 Listen and complete these sentences.**

The missing words all begin with a consonant cluster.

a)   It burns with a blue _____ .

b)   There was a _____ rise in crime.

c)   We are on _____ for ten per cent _____ this year.

d)   We need a more _____ definition of the term.

e) It's covered with a steel _____ .

f) The _____ needs replacing.

g) Its development can be _____ back to the 15th century.

h) The screen went _____ .

i) There is _____ evidence for such a link.

j) It's difficult to follow the _____ of his argument.

1.3 Listen again and repeat the phrases. Try to focus on the correct pronunciation of the consonant cluster, on the correct word stress and on linking.

1.4 CD2 – 22 Listen and repeat these further examples of consonant clusters which begin with /s/.

scale	sleep	spare	split	straight
scheme	slip	spill	splendid	stress
scope	slight	speed		strike
score	slope	spoil	stage	strong
		specific	step	
screen	smart		store	sweet
script	smell	spray	stuff	swing
	smoke	spread	style	switch
snack	smooth	spring		
snow				

1.5 CD2 – 23 Listen and complete these phrases or sentences.

The missing words all begin with /s/ and a consonant cluster.

a) This machine _____ the brain.

b) Resources are _____ .

c) This _____ is under threat.

d) We're making _____ progress.

e) one important _____

f) He _____ paint on the floor.

g) a _____ feeling

h) a bigger _____ of the cake

i) in a _____ condition

j) a _____ floor

1.6 Listen again and repeat the phrases or sentences. Try to focus on the correct pronunciation of the consonant cluster, on the correct word stress and on linking.

Task 2: Consonant clusters in the middle of words

2.1 ⊙ **CD2 – 24 Listen and repeat these words, which include consonant clusters.**

impress	central	explain	include	abstract
comprise	contract	exploit	conclude	construct
compromise	control	explore	enclose	distribute
complain	entry	explicit	unclear	industry
complete	introduce			illustrate
employ	inspect	extract	conflict	
sample	transport	extreme	influence	
			inflation	

2.2 ⊙ **CD2 – 25 Listen and complete these phrases or sentences with words from Ex 2.1.**

a) Supplies need to be _____.

b) no _____ reference

c) the _____ infrastructure

d) this _____ with

e) The causes are _____.

f) oils _____ from plants

g) an _____ concept

h) in order to _____ its potential fully

i) It _____ three parts.

j) in _____ cases

2.3 **Listen again and repeat the phrases or sentences. Try to focus on the correct pronunciation of the consonant cluster, on the correct word stress and on linking.**

Task 3: Disappearing sounds in connected speech

3.1 ⊙ **CD2 – 26 Listen to these sentences and write in the word that is missing.**

a) Did _____ tell you?

b) I've added _____ name to the list.

c) Can you put _____ suitcase in the car?

When function words beginning with *h*, like *he, his, him, her*, are *unstressed* and in the *middle* of a sentence, the /h/ sound often disappears.

However, if these words are at the *beginning* of a sentence, the /h/ sound is usually pronounced, e.g., *He left at four o'clock.*

Contractions of auxiliary and modal verbs

In connected speech, auxiliary verbs and some modal verbs are often contracted; that is to say, some of the sounds disappear when they are unstressed. Here is a list of some of the most common contractions.

Full form	Contraction	Full form	Contraction
he is / he has she is / she has they are they have	he's she's they're they've	could have should have must have	could've should've must've
it would / it had he would / he had	it'd he'd	is not are not will not can not would not	isn't aren't won't can't wouldn't

Note:
1 In academic writing, you should use the full forms and not the contracted forms.
2 *he's* might represent *he is* or *he has,* depending on context.
3 *he'd* might represent *he had* or *he would,* depending on context.

3.2 ⊙ **CD2 – 27 Listen and complete the sentences.**

Note: There are two or three words missing from each space.

a) Although _____ requested further funding, _____ not certain that the project will continue beyond 2005.

b) The treatment is expensive, and _____ why _____ not very widely available.

c) Another advantage is that _____ lower the costs.

d) In fact, _____ supposed to be checked every six months.

e) We _____ know for sure, but _____ thought that the space probe _____ been hit by a meteorite.

f) Unfortunately, _____ forgotten just how complicated the process is.

g) The Vikings are believed _____ landed in America well before Columbus.

h) The equipment testing _____ been left until the last minute.

3.3 ⊙ **CD2 – 28 Listen to these words and phrases and, in the words in bold, cross out the vowels that are not pronounced.**

Note: Unstressed short vowels in some words sometimes disappear, too.

Example: *comfortable* is often pronounced /ˈkʌmftəbəl/, so the letters ~or~ are not pronounced.

a) **Vegetables** are grown on about 60 per cent of farms in the area.

b) **Perhaps** he's left.

c) Which **category** does it fit in?

d) She's studying **medicine**.

e) I'll phone her **secretary**.

3.4   ⊚ **CD2 – 29 Listen to the sentences a–f, paying particular attention to the consonant clusters in the words in bold. Cross out the consonants that are not pronounced.**

Where you have groups of consonants together (consonant clusters), some consonants may disappear to make them easier to pronounce in normal informal speech.

Example: *next month* is pronounced /neks mʌnθ/, so the letter *t* may disappear.

a) It **reacts** with sulphur.

b) They'll **send** back the results on Tuesday.

c) It **must** be checked.

d) The low election turnout **reflects** growing apathy towards politics.

e) It has some **good points**.

f) The engine **tends** to overheat in particular circumstances.

Generally, as in the above examples, the consonants *t* and *d* are only dropped when they are trapped between other consonants, rather than vowels.

Task 4: Tone units

Whereas written English is split into words, spoken English is split into what are known as tone units. Each tone unit contains at least one prominent syllable. If, however, it contains two, then it is usually the second that contains the main sentence stress. This is the tonic syllable, and it is where most of the pitch change takes place.

4.1   ⊚ **CD2 – 30 Listen to someone speaking the above text and notice how it is split into tone units.**

Whereas **writ**ten **Eng**lish // is split into **words** // **spok**en English // is **split** into what are **known** // as **tone** units //. Each **tone un**it // contains at least one **prom**inent **syl**lable //. If, how**ev**er, // it contains **two** //, then it is **u**sually the **se**cond // which contains the **main** sentence **stress** //. This is the **ton**ic **syl**lable // and it is where **most** of the **pitch change** // **takes place** //.

4.2   ⊚ **CD2 – 31 Listen to part of the lecture entitled *An Introduction to British Agriculture*. Mark the tone units by writing in double slash signs (//) in the right places.**

You will find it helpful to listen for brief pauses and changes in speaker key.

> As a backdrop to all of these activities, particularly after the Second World War, a lot of effort was put into research and development of agriculture in terms of plant breeding, breeding crops that were higher yielding, that were perhaps disease-resistant, and so on and so forth. Also, crops that might have better quality, better bread-making quality, higher gluten content to make them doughy, higher protein content, and so on and so forth. Research, too, and this is again at one of the university farms, research into livestock production. Understanding how to better manage our livestock, again to make them produce more, certainly, but also to produce and influence the quality of the livestock products, whether that happens to be milk or cheese, come back to that in a moment, or indeed meat.

4.3 🎧 **CD2 – 32 Now listen to an extract from the lecture on globalization. Mark the tone units by writing in double slash signs (//) in the right places.**

Now to get to the the meat of the lecture, the basic purpose of this lecture is to give you some overview of the kind of contemporary academic and policy debate about globalization and particularly about a very specific, although rather general debate itself, that is the debate on the effect of globalization on the role of the state. So you see on the overhead the lecture's going to be kind of in two parts: the first will be looking at globalization, causes and consequences and more particularly a kind of definition of the discussion of some of the competing conceptions of globalization, that is, y'know, what people say it is, so that we can then discuss in some detail hopefully this question of how globalization's affecting the state.

Unit Summary

In this unit, you have focused on the correct pronunciation of consonant clusters at the beginning and in the middle of words. You have also looked at sounds that disappear in connected speech and have become more aware of how English speech is divided into tone units.

1   🎧 **CD2 – 33 Listen to how the following words are pronounced. Say the words in each group below. Underline any words that you find difficult to pronounce.**

a) spare	spoil	speed	spray
b) central	entry	quarter	track
c) school	scale	share	scheme
d) street	store	stress	straight
e) complete	complex	construct	comprise
f) abstract	industry	construct	inspect

2   **Identify the consonant cluster in each word.**

3   **Decide which word you think is the odd one out in each group.**

Note: There may be more than one possible answer.

4   **Read the text and then answer the questions below.**

You have got some interesting ideas and make some good points, but you could have developed these a bit more. You must make sure that you check your essay for spelling mistakes and check the grammar is correct. Perhaps you should have asked your tutor to read through your work, as he would have helped you improve it.

a)   🎧 **CD2 – 34** Listen to someone speaking the above text and mark the tone units.

b)   Try to read the text aloud as you listen to the recording, paying attention to the consonant clusters and tone units.

For web resources, see:

www.englishforacademicstudy.com/student/pronunciation/links

These weblinks will provide you with further practice in areas of pronunciation such as the sounds, stress and intonation patterns of English.

In this unit you will:
- learn which phonemic symbols represent other diphthongs;
- practise recognizing and producing these diphthongs;
- have more practice identifying sentence stress and tone units.

Diphthongs

In this unit, you will focus on the diphthongs shaded in this table.

/aɪ/	/aʊ/	/əʊ/	/eɪ/	/eə/	/ɪə/	/ɔɪ/	/ʊə/
wh<u>y</u>	n<u>ow</u>	g<u>o</u>	d<u>ay</u>	c<u>are</u>	d<u>ear</u>	enj<u>oy</u>	p<u>ure</u>

Task 1: /eə/ and /ɪə/

1.1 🎧 **CD2 – 35 Put the words in the box into the correct column of the table, according to the pronunciation of the diphthong sound.**

> share   fair   mere   square   near   adhere   sphere   year   there   where
> aware   appear   severe   wear   pair   chair   bear   fare

/eə/	/ɪə/

Pronunciation note

The /eə/ sound is often written as:

- ~are: care, prepare;
- ~air: hair, repair.

The /ɪə/ sound is often written as:

- ~ear: fear, gear;
- ~ere: here, sincere.

However, there are exceptions to these patterns, e.g., wear /weə/, bear /beə/, where /weə/ and there /ðeə/.

1.2 Check how your answers to Ex 1.1 fit these patterns.

1.3 ⊚ CD2 – 36 **Using words from Ex 1.1, complete these sentences by writing in the missing words.**

a) As far as I'm _____ , there has been little previous research into this issue.

b) Patients suffering from _____ depression are often treated with drugs.

c) The _____ fact that they have agreed to negotiate does not indicate that an end to the conflict is near.

d) These countries needed to _____ for entry into the EMU.

e) How can we _____ the damage done?

f) The area of land is about 20 metres _____ .

g) The seeds _____ to the fur of animals, which distribute them over a large area.

h) We need to _____ in mind that events in South America are largely beyond the UK's _____ of influence.

Listen again and repeat.

Task 2: /aʊ/ and /əʊ/

2.1 ⊚ CD2 – 37 **Put the words in the box into the correct column of the table, according to the pronunciation of _ow_.**

allow	crowd	below	own	flow	down	power	growth	now	know
slow	follow	brown	show	powder	crown	owe	shower		

/aʊ/	/əʊ/

Note: The letters _ow_ are sometimes pronounced /aʊ/ and sometimes /əʊ/.

2.2 🎧 CD2 – 38 **Underline the words below which include the /aʊ/ sound.**

Note: The letters *ou* are often also pronounced /aʊ/, but not always.

loud	doubt	group	account	court	serious	sound	various	trouble
south	amount	colour	course	enough	young	hour	ground	flavour

2.3 🎧 CD2 – 39 **Listen and complete the sentences, using words from Exs 2.1 and 2.2.**

a) How do we _____ for this increase in temperature?

b) Margaret Thatcher came to _____ in 1979.

c) The new road system is designed to improve traffic _____ through the city centre.

d) The animal feed is usually sold in _____ form.

e) It is without _____ the most _____ crisis the government has faced.

f) You need to _____ 21 days for delivery.

g) Economic _____ has slowed down over the last six months.

h) He is doing research into _____ behaviour.

i) A significant _____ of water is lost through perspiration.

j) The cheese has quite a strong _____ .

Listen again and repeat.

Task 3: /ɔɪ/

3.1 🎧 CD2 – 40 **Listen and repeat the following words.**

Note: The letters *oi* and *oy* are usually pronounced /ɔɪ/.

coin	point	join	avoid	soil	noise
boy	employ	enjoy	royal	annoy	soya

3.2 🎧 CD2 – 41 **Listen and complete these sentences by writing a word in each space.**

Note: Each word includes the letters *oi* or *oy*, but they are not words from the previous exercise.

a) The questionnaire comprises multiple-_____ and open questions.

b) The government is keen for parents to have a _____ in determining how their children are educated.

c) During the civil war, the army remained _____ to the king.

d) The company has _____ a new marketing director.

e) Large parts of the city were _____ in the earthquake.

f) It is often claimed that we fail to _____ scientific developments made in UK universities.

g) Many sailors died during long sea _____ because of poor nutrition.

h) The new company is a _____ venture between Italian and Egyptian _____ companies.

Listen again and repeat.

Task 4: Tone units 2

4.1 **CD2 – 42 Listen and complete this lecture on higher education in England and Wales. Write one to five words in each space.**

... in Britain, _____ do that _____
to tell you something about the education _____ before students
_____ level. There are _____ reasons for this.
_____ it's part of the plan of your course _____
to give you the experience of lectures before you go into your real departments in September
or October, _____ is that we have found _____
_____ that many students come to Britain and they live and study here _____
_____ and they go away without knowing _____
most basic facts about the education system here. It's _____ that the
education system here, _____ your countries, is changing very rapidly,
and this means _____ people, you know, people as old as me, who
don't _____ have direct _____, they probably
give you information about the education system as _____ rather
than as it _____ is now.

Now what qualifications, _____, do I have to speak on this particular
_____? Well, I'm, _____ in the introduction, I'm
here at Reading University and my main _____ is to look after
international students here, like you, who need academic language support. Now between
20 and 23 per cent of the students in this university, in Reading University, do not have
English as their first language and did not receive their previous education in the United
Kingdom. So that's a large number of students, _____ almost two
and a half thousand students, in this university were not _____
educated in the United Kingdom before they came to university, so you are amongst many.
_____ a minority, but you're a very large minority.

4.2 **Listen again and mark the tone units in Ex 4.1 by writing in double slash signs (//) in the right places. Look back to Unit 6, Task 4, for an explanation of tone units.**

4.3 ⊚ **CD2 – 43 Listen to this excerpt from a lecture titled** *Financial Markets and Instruments* **and decide where the sentence stress falls.**

Well, the title, *Financial Markets and Instruments,* what are we going to do here? Well, we're going to start by explaining why we need a financial market at all. What is the role that is played by a financial market? What is the rationale for having a financial market? And then we're going to move on and explain some of the instruments that are traded in those markets, some of the instruments that I was saying you are familiar with already, because they are simply stocks, bonds, bills: money market instruments. If you've done any finance before, you might be familiar also with the other ones, which are future swap options, which are derivative instruments, and I'm going to focus mainly on the stocks, bonds, bills, since these are by far the easiest to understand. OK, let's start with a simple definition, and I guess anyone here could have given this definition on their own: what is a financial market? Well, a financial market is a market where financial securities are traded. Nothing very very tricky here.

4.4 **Listen again and mark the tone units in Ex 4.3 by writing in double slash signs (//) in the right places.**

Unit Summary

In this unit, you have learnt the phonemic symbols for the diphthongs /eə/, /ɪə/, /aʊ/ and /ɔɪ/ and looked at sound/spelling patterns for words that contain them. You have also had more practice in identifying sentence stress and tone units.

1 Each of the words in the box contains one of the diphthongs in the table below. Write them in the correct column.

> annoy   square   crowd   growth   severe   soya   although   doubt
> steer   owe   pair   south   bear   avoid   year

eə	ɪə	aʊ	əʊ	ɔɪ

🎧 CD2 – 44 **Listen and check your answers.**

2 Write three more words for each column. Choose words from the unit or from your area of study.

3 Study the different spelling patterns for each sound. Are there any exceptions to the patterns that you looked at in the unit?

4 Read the statements below and decide whether you agree with each one or not.

a) English words can be hard to pronounce because there are so many vowel sounds and spelling patterns.

b) Looking at the phonemes for the vowel or diphthong sounds in a new word helps me remember its pronunciation.

c) It is important to understand how native speakers join words together and omit sounds when they speak in English.

d) It is less important for non-native speakers to use connected speech features themselves.

e) It is easier to understand a talk or lecture if you are aware of how the speaker divides his or her speech into tone units.

For web resources, see:
www.englishforacademicstudy.com/student/pronunciation/links

These weblinks will provide you with further practice in areas of pronunciation such as the sounds, stress and intonation patterns of English.

8 Consonant clusters 2, intonation

In this unit you will:
- learn how to pronounce consonant clusters at the end of words and across two words;
- learn how intonation is used to organize and emphasize information.

Task 1: Consonant clusters

In Unit 6, you studied consonant clusters at the beginning and in the middle of words. In this unit, you will learn how to pronounce consonant clusters at the end of words and across two words.

1.1   🅰 **CD2 – 45 Listen and repeat these groups of words, which end with consonant clusters.**

Note: In some cases, you may hear a very short /ə/ between the consonants. A word like *arrival* may be pronounced as /əˈraɪvl/ or as /əˈraɪvəl/.

arrival	impact	criticism	depth	branch
critical	conflict	mechanism	length	lunch
external	affect	organism	strength	launch
financial	abstract	tourism	width	bench
principal			wealth	
	range	eleven		
assemble	arrange	given		
resemble	change	govern		
	challenge	driven		

1.2   🅰 **CD2 – 46 Listen to these phrases and sentences and write the missing words in the spaces.**

Note: All the words end in consonant clusters.

a) in the _____ stage

b) The job has some _____ benefits.

c) I've lost a _____ of keys.

d) a rather _____ surface

e) It was discussed at some _____.

f) This is a key _____ of his work.

g) He's studying _____ at Leeds University.

h) They can't afford to take such a _____.

i) the _____ of investment controls

j) in the _____ grade

1.3 ⊙ **CD2 – 47 Listen to the past verb forms in the box and put them in the correct column of the table, depending on the pronunciation of ~ed.**

Note: Simple past and past participle forms of regular verbs are formed by adding ~ed, and this ending is pronounced /t/, /d/ or /ɪd/, depending on the verb.

equipped   combined   involved   concluded   constructed
depended   developed   expressed   claimed   advised   arranged
adapted   lacked   finished   absorbed

/t/ or /d/	/ɪd/

Pronunciation note

When the infinitive form ends in /t/ or /d/, you add /ɪd/.

Examples:

want	⟶	wanted
vote	⟶	voted
avoid	⟶	avoided
decide	⟶	decided

When the infinitive ends with any other *unvoiced* consonant, you add /t/.

Examples:

stop	⟶	stopped
pick	⟶	picked
push	⟶	pushed

When the infinitive ends with any other *voiced* consonant, a vowel or a diphthong, you add /d/.

Examples:

try	⟶	tried
tag	⟶	tagged
tamper	⟶	tampered

In Unit 6, Ex 3.4, we listened to examples of how the consonants *t* and *d* are dropped when they are trapped between other consonants. Sometimes, dropping *t* and *d* can eliminate the distinction between present simple and past simple verb forms, which means that the examples in Ex 1.4 are likely to sound the same.

1.4   ⊙ **CD2 – 48 Listen to the following examples.**

> I watch television every night.

and

> I watched television last night.

or

> Many suppliers raise their prices in situations like this.

and

> Many suppliers raised their prices when the exchange rate rose.

These examples show that, when listening, you need to compare what you hear with your understanding of the context, to make sure that you correctly decode meaning.

Pronunciation note

If you find it difficult to pronounce the consonant clusters, try imagining that the final consonant is part of the following word.

For example, if you find it difficult to say *It lacked a clear focus*, try saying *It lack ta clear focus*.

1.5   ⊙ **CD2 – 49 Listen and repeat these phrases.**

a) arranged at short notice

b) the team involved in the project

c) it was constructed in three months

d) it's absorbed into the bloodstream

e) the benefits claimed in the report

f) we've avoided the problem

g) a technique developed in Brazil

h) specially adapted equipment

i) aimed at a niche market

j) enclosed in plastic

Task 2: Intonation

2.1   ⊙ **CD2 – 50 Listen to the following short exchange.**

A: Has everything been checked?

B: Yes, I think so.

A: What about the ↓temperature?

B: Yes, I've checked the ↑temperature, and it's normal.

In the last two lines, the word *temperature* is stressed. However, if you listen carefully, you will hear that the voice goes down in tone in the first instance (*falling intonation*) and up in tone in the second instance (*rising intonation*).

Listen to the two words in isolation.

A: ↓temperature

B: ↑temperature

2.2 ⊙ **CD2 – 51 Listen to another short exchange and do the three activities below.**

A: It's too expensive.

B: Well, it's expensive, but it's worth it.

a) Underline the word that is stressed in each sentence.

b) Note whether there is a rising (↑) or falling (↓) intonation on the stressed words.

c) Listen again and check your answers.

Pronunciation note

In English, speakers use intonation for different functions. The main ones come under these two categories:

- to organize and emphasize information;
- to show their attitude to the topic under discussion.

Like sentence stress, changes of intonation are affected by speaker choice and context. They are not governed by a clear set of rules.

In the exchanges in Exs 2.1 and 2.2, the reasons for the choice of intonation patterns are as follows:

- a *falling tone*, e.g., ↓*temperature*, is generally used when the speaker *introduces a new idea into the discussion*;
- a *rising tone*, e.g., ↑*temperature*, is generally used when the speaker *refers to an idea that has already been introduced*. In other words, it is <u>not</u> a new idea in the discussion.

A falling intonation is generally used when a conclusion has been reached.

In sentence 4 of Ex 2.1 ,this occurs on the word *normal*, which therefore has a falling tone: *I've checked the ↑temperature, and it's ↓normal.*

2.3 ⊙ **CD2 – 52 Compare this conversation with the previous one.**

Note: Even when we use different words to refer back to a previous idea, there is still a rising intonation.

A: It's too ↓**expensive**.

B: Yes, it's a lot of ↑**money**, but it's ↓worth it.

In this case, *money* has a rising tone because it refers back to the idea of *expensive*.

2.4 ⊙ **CD2 – 53 Listen to these short conversations. Notice the falling intonation for new information and the rising tone for information that is not new.**

a) **A:** When's the ↓**deadline** for the new building project?

   B: The ↑**deadline**? I think it's next Thursday.

b) **A:** Why do these prices ↓**fluctuate**?

   B: Changes in the exchange rate cause this ↑**variation**.

2.5 ⊙ **CD2 – 54 Listen to this conversation and mark the falling and rising intonation.**

Note: The rise or fall starts on the stressed word and continues to the end of the tone unit (see page 53). The first rise has been marked for you as an example. The stressed words are in bold.

A: Can I ↑**help** you?

B: Yes, where's the **Physics** Department?

A: It's on the second **floor**.

B: On the **second** floor?

A: Yes, that's right. Take the **lift** over there.

B: I'm not keen on **lifts**. I'd rather **walk** there.

A: Suit yourself. The **stairs** are down the **corridor**, on the **left**.

B: **Down there**, on the **left**. Thanks very much!

2.6 **Now take the role of Student B and reply to Student A in the pauses provided.**

2.7 ⊙ **CD2 – 55 Listen to this short extract from a lecture and think about the use of intonation.**

> In these two lectures, we're going to look at two theories of child **development**. Firstly, I'm going to look at Jean **Piaget**. Then, next week, I'll talk about the life and work of Erick **Erickson**. So this week, it's about Jean **Piaget**. Now Piaget's theories were very much influenced by his own experiences, so I'm going to talk about his life and how he developed his ideas, and then I'm going to describe Piaget's four stages of child **development**.

2.8 **What is the lecturer signalling by his use of falling intonation on the words in bold?**

Note: When we are listening to lectures, we need to understand how the lecturer signals what he is going to say through his use of intonation.

2.9 ☉ **CD2 – 56** Listen to a student talking about the advantages and disadvantages of streaming video from a website and mark the rising and falling tones on the stressed words in bold.

> With **streaming** video, the video is **downloaded** to your **computer** as you are **listening** to it. And usually you can't **save** it.
>
> This **stops** people making **copies** of the video, **editing** or **pirating** it.
>
> The **problem** is, if you don't have enough **bandwidth**, or if you're on a **network** and it's very **busy**, your **computer** won't be able to download **fast** enough.
>
> As a **result**, the picture quality is often **poor**, or the pictures are **jerky**. Sometimes, the video even **freezes**.

2.10 Think about the use of falling and rising tones in the previous audio extracts. Did a falling tone signal the speaker was introducing a new idea and a rising tone signal the speaker was referring to an idea that had already been introduced, as suggested in the previous Pronunciation note?

If you were listening carefully, you may have picked up examples of a more subtle phenomenon, the fall–rise, used where there is no back reference, e.g., *firstly* or *next week*.

2.11 Listen again to Tracks 55 and 56. Can you recall any other examples?

2.12 ☉ **CD2 – 57** Listen again to the first dialogue in Ex 2.1.

As mentioned in the previous note, intonation, or tone of voice, is also used to show the speaker's attitude. It is for this purpose that the fall–rise is most often employed. If you were listening carefully, you may have picked this up already.

A: Has everything been ↓↑checked? (conveying concern)

B: Yes, I ↓↑think so. (But I'm not sure – conveying uncertainty.)

Consider also:

A: He's an ↓excellent ↓↑speaker. (But does he have any new ideas?)

B: I ↓know what you ↓↑mean. (But I'm not sure you are being fair. He has some good ideas.)

In this example, the fall–rise is used to indicate that 'more can be said'.

2.13 ☉ **CD2 – 58** Listen and compare the speakers' intonation in a) and b). Which one would you generally expect of an offer of help?

a) Can I ↑help you?

b) Can I ↓↑help you? (a more polite and friendly offer)

2.14 🎧 **CD2 – 59 Finally, consider the function of the fall–rise in the following:**

A: We need to improve the ↑**technology**.

B: But training is just as important as ↓↑**technology**.

A: That's just your ↓**opinion**.

B: It's not just an ↓↑**opinion**. There's evidence to support it.

Here, the fall–rise is used by speaker B to indicate a viewpoint that is in some way different from speaker A's.

Unit Summary

In this unit, you have focused on the correct pronunciation of consonant clusters at the end of words and across two words. You have also looked at how intonation is used to organize and emphasize information.

1 **Complete the summary below, using your own words.**

Consonant clusters

- Sometimes, consonant sounds can disappear when

  _____

  _____

  e.g., _____

- *-ed* past forms of regular verbs can be pronounced in three different ways:

  _____

  _____

  e.g., _____

- If you find consonant clusters difficult to pronounce, try

  _____

  _____

  e.g., _____

2   🎧 **CD2 – 60 Listen to the dialogue and mark the rising and falling tones on the stressed words marked in bold.**

A: We need to discuss your **essay**. Can you come to my office at **3.00**?

B: I've got a lecture at **3.00**. And I think I'm working in the **evening**.

A: How about **tomorrow**? I'll be there at **lunchtime**.

B: OK. I'll come **then**.

3   **Think about what you have learnt about pronunciation while studying this book and try to answer the questions below.**

a) Which aspects of English pronunciation have you become more aware of while working through this book?

b) How has this helped you when you listen to English speakers?

c) Which aspects of your own pronunciation have you worked on and/or improved most?

d) What sort of tasks and exercises have you found most useful?

e) Which aspects of your pronunciation are you still concerned about?

f) What can you do to continue to work on these areas?

> For web resources, see:
>
> **www.englishforacademicstudy.com/student/pronunciation/links**
>
> These weblinks will provide you with further practice in areas of pronunciation such as the sounds, stress and intonation patterns of English.

g Glossary

Academic Word List (AWL)
A list of 570 word families that are most commonly used in academic contexts.

Connected speech
The stream of words that form the normal pattern of spoken language. It is important to note that words are pronounced differently in connected speech than when they are in isolation.

Consonant
A speech sound made by blocking or partly blocking the air used to make the sound, e.g., blocked /b/ or partly blocked (through the nose) /ŋ/.

Consonant clusters
Groups of consonants that occur together at the beginning, in the middle of or at the end of words, e.g., _grow_, _congratulate_, _tracks_.

Diphthong
A sound that involves two vowels joined together, e.g., the /aɪ/ sound in _why_. A diphthong is treated as one sound and given a single phonemic symbol.

Falling tone/falling intonation
A downward change in tone (or pitch) that gives the listener more understanding of what the speaker is saying. A falling tone generally indicates finality and certainty, and is often used when the speaker is giving new information.

Function words
Words that have no concrete meaning, but convey grammatical relationships between words, e.g., articles, conjunctions, prepositions.

General Service List (GSL)
The 2,000 most frequently used words in English.

Intonation
The way a speaker raises and lowers her/his tone of voice (or pitch) to clarify meaning. Intonation is used to show attitude or emotion and to clarify discourse and grammatical features.

Micro-skills
Skills that enable the learner to piece together small pieces of information to build a bigger picture and make sense of something. A study of pronunciation helps to develop listening and speaking micro-skills.

Phonemic alphabet
A written set of symbols used to represent the sounds of individual languages.

Phonemic symbol
A symbol that is used to represent an individual sound. The main sounds of English are represented by 44 phonemic symbols.

Phonemic transcription
The use of phonemic symbols to show the sounds of speech in written form. It provides the learner with an indication of how a native speaker would pronounce a word, or longer stretches of speech.

Pronunciation
The way sounds are produced to form speech; it covers the individual sounds, the way some sounds are stressed, and the intonation patterns within utterances.

Rising tone/rising intonation
An upward change in tone (or pitch) that gives the listener more understanding of what the speaker is saying. A rising tone generally indicates that the topic or utterance is unfinished, or that the speaker is referring to shared information that has already been introduced.

Sentence stress
The way certain words in a sentence are spoken with more force, also called *prominence*.

Sound/spelling patterns
The connection between the sounds of a language and the way they are spelt. English does not have a one-to-one relationship between sounds and spelling, but there are many useful patterns that will help the speaker.

Suffix
A letter or group of letters that can be added to the end of a word to change its meaning. Words with similar suffixes often have similar stress patterns. Suffixes that come at the end of adjectives include ~*tial*, ~*cial* and ~*ical*.

Syllable
A unit of sound within a word. Each syllable has a vowel at its centre, and consonants may 'surround' the vowel. It is also possible to have a syllable with just a vowel. For example, one-syllable words: *post*, *take*, two-syllable words: *o•mit, pro•vide, ques•tion*.

Tone unit
A stretch of spoken language that includes at least one prominent syllable which marks the beginning of a change in intonation pattern.

Unvoiced consonant
When pronouncing unvoiced consonants, the vocal chords in your throat do not vibrate, e.g., /p/, /t/ and /k/.

Voiced consonant
When pronouncing voiced consonants, the vocal chords in your throat vibrate, e.g., /b/, /d/ and /g/.

Vowel
A speech sound made without blocking the air used to produce the sound. Variations in vowel sounds are determined mainly by the shape of the mouth, how open the mouth is and the position of the tongue.

Weak form
When a word changes its pronunciation according to whether it is stressed or not, the unstressed version is known as a weak form. Using a weak form affects the vowel sounds within the word, e.g., *for* is pronounced /fə/ in a weak form.

Word family
A group of words that have the same basic form and similar meanings. For example, the words *produce, product, production* and *unproductive* are all in the same word family.

Word stress
This is the way that one syllable in a word is given more force. Stressed syllables are louder and longer than unstressed syllables.

Transcripts

Unit 1: Vowel sounds 1, word stress and weak forms

◉CD1, Track 1

Ex 1.1
Listen to the difference in the pronunciation of these pairs of words. In each of them, the vowel sound is different.

a)

fit	feet
dip	deep
hit	heat

b)

mass	mess
band	bend
had	head

c)

hat	heart
match	march
pack	park

d)

ten	turn
head	heard
went	weren't

◉CD1, Track 2

Ex 1.2
You will hear some of the words from Ex 1.1. Listen and circle the phonemic transcription that matches the pronunciation of the word you hear.

Example: heard

a) park
b) turn
c) mass
d) heat
e) weren't
f) deep
g) head
h) heart
i) band

◉CD1, Track 3

Ex 1.3
Listen to six more words and do the following exercises.

a) Listen and circle the phonemic transcription that matches the pronunciation of the word you hear.

1 seat
2 met
3 hurt
4 fur
5 live
6 sad

◉CD1, Track 4

Ex 2.1
Listen to these examples of words with one, two and three or more syllables.

a) one-syllable words

aid
quote
source
fee

b) two-syllable words

credit
accept
heavy
equate

c) words with three or more syllables

policy
similar
environment
identify
individual

⊕CD1, Track 5

Ex 2.2
Listen to these words and decide how many syllables there are in each of them.

a) specific

b) alter

c) resource

d) preliminary

e) available

f) consequent

g) framework

h) significant

i) adapt

j) differentiate

⊕CD1, Track 6

Ex 3.1
Listen for the stressed syllable in these words.

policy

similar

environment

identify

individual

assume

major

overseas

operation

reinforce

⊕CD1, Track 7

Ex 3.2
Listen again to the words from Ex 2.2. Mark the stressed syllables as shown in the following example.

a) specific

b) alter

c) resource

d) preliminary

e) available

f) consequent

g) framework

h) significant

i) adapt

j) differentiate

⊕CD1, Track 8

Ex 3.3
Listen to the following sentences and mark the stressed syllable in the words in bold.

a) The **protection** of children is the main purpose of this legislation.

b) The samples were **analyzed** in the lab.

c) Chemical **analysis** of the rock provided surprising results.

d) The aim of the study was to **identify** the **factors** contributing to domestic violence.

e) **Periodicals** are kept in an area on the ground floor.

f) The **administration** of these drugs needs to be closely monitored.

g) In **percentage** terms, this is not a significant increase.

h) This is the standard **procedure** for limiting spread of the disease.

⊕CD1, Track 9

Ex 4.1
Listen to these pairs of sentences. What is the difference in the pronunciation of the words in bold in each pair? How can you explain this difference?

a) 1 Interest rates **are** rising. (weak form)

  2 No, that's not true. We **are** doing something about it. (strong form)

b) 1 Would you like **some** tea? (weak form)

  2 Most scientists are convinced about global warming, but **some** are not. (strong form)

c) 1 Where's he coming **from**? (strong form)

  2 Results differed **from** one region to another. (weak form)

d) 1 Is that **your** pen or mine? (strong form)

  2 Can I borrow **your** dictionary? (weak form)

⊕CD1, Track 10

Ex 4.2
Listen to these sentences and write in the missing words, which are all weak forms of function words.

a) One criticism levelled at the board was their lack of financial control.

b) This issue was discussed at some length during the conference.

c) These points should have been made more effectively.

d) How do we account for this change in behaviour?

e) This might do more harm than good.

f) This kind of restructuring is usually regarded by employees as a change for the worse.

g) This problem can easily be solved at minimal cost.

h) Trade sanctions will be imposed with effect from the 1st of December.

Ex 4.3
Study the following introduction to a lecture on globalization. Then listen and write in the missing words, which again are weak forms of function words.

Well, as Ros said, I'm going to talk about globalization today, which is one of the catch phrases or buzzwords, if you like, of the late 20th and early 21st centuries. It's constantly in the news. It's used by politicians, by people in the media, by business people, and when they're referring to globalization they talk about things like the way we can communicate almost instantaneously nowadays with people on the other side of the world by e-mail or by television. They're also talking about, for example, the way that a fall in share prices in one part of the world, for example in the Far East, can have an immediate impact on the stock markets on the other side of the world, like in London or Frankfurt.

⊚CD1, Track 12

Ex 4.4
Listen to these phrases and repeat them. Can you identify and produce the weak forms of the function words?

a) past and present figures
b) more or less fifty
c) they were selected at random
d) it was far from clear
e) the results of the trials
f) too good to be true
g) needless to say
h) it's gone from bad to worse
i) we'll have to wait and see
j) we had some problems

Unit 1 Summary

⊚CD1, Track 13

Ex 2
Now listen to the words from Ex 1 and mark the stressed syllable in each word.

globalization
century
constantly
politician
refer
media
financial
market

Unit 2: Vowel sounds 2, word stress patterns

⊚CD1, Track 14

Ex 1.1
Listen to the difference in the pronunciation of these pairs of words. In each of them, the vowel sound is different.

a)

match	much
lack	luck
ankle	uncle

b)

pull	pool
soot	suit
full	fool

c)

spot	sport
shot	short
stock	stalk

d)

lock	look
box	books
shock	shook

⊚CD1, Track 15

Ex 1.2
You will hear some of the words from Ex 1.1. Listen and circle the phonemic transcription that matches the pronunciation of the word you hear.

Example: lack

a) books
b) pool
c) spit
d) match
e) uncle
f) fool
g) luck
h) stock
i) short

⊚CD1, Track 16

Ex 1.3
Listen to six more words and do the following exercises.

a) **Listen and circle the phonemic transcription that matches the pronunciation of the word you hear.**

1   fun
2   mud
3   cool
4   bought
5   foot
6   card

Ex 2.1
Listen to these examples.

appear
suggest
effort
colour

Ex 2.2
c) Listen and repeat the words.

Example: computer

1   affect
2   several
3   standard
4   failure
5   purpose
6   propose
7   author
8   attempt
9   distance
10 accept
11 opposite
12 flavour
13 compare
14 approach

Ex 2.3
Listen to these examples.

describe
prefer

Ex 2.4
c) Listen and repeat the words.

Example: reduce

1   invited
2   decision
3   demand
4   beyond

5   extensive
6   research
7   interpret

Ex 3.1
Listen and repeat the following words, making sure you stress the syllables in the columns highlighted in the tables below.

Nouns ending in ~sion or ~tion

discussion
solution
occasion
definition
decision
position

Nouns ending in ~graphy

geography
biography
photography

Adjectives ending in ~ic

electric
economic
specific

Nouns ending in ~ency or ~ancy

frequency
consultancy
consistency
vacancy
efficiency
redundancy

Nouns ending in ~ium

medium
uranium
consortium

Adjectives ending in ~ical

electrical
political
periodical

Nouns ending in ~ity

identity
authority
community

Adjectives ending in ~tial or ~cial

essential
financial
potential
commercial
residential
artificial

Verbs ending in ~ify

modify
clarify
identify

Nouns ending in ~logy

apology
technology
biology

Adjectives ending in ~tional

additional
international
optional

⊕CD1, Track 22

Ex 3.2
b) Listen to check your answers. Repeat the words to practise your pronunciation.

1   academic
2   dimension
3   beneficial
4   similarity
5   majority
6   initial
7   demography
8   allergic
9   tradition
10   deficiency
11   conventional
12   justify

⊕CD1, Track 23

Ex 3.3
Now listen to check your answers.

a)   Most of the course modules are compulsory, but there are two optional modules.

b)   The committee has not yet taken a decision whether or not to award funding for the project.

c)   It is important to start with a definition of the term 'sustainable development', as it clearly means different things to different people.

d)   Although solar power provides a potential answer to some of the world's energy needs, at the moment the technology is quite expensive.

e)   Have we really found a solution to the problem?

f)   It is hoped that the development of artificial intelligence will mean that computers will be able to think in the way humans do.

g)   There is a lot of confusion, so it is essential to clarify the situation.

h)   The stadium was built by an international consortium of construction companies.

i)   There is a vacancy for a laboratory technician, so the post will be advertized next week.

j)   James Watson's biography of Margaret Thatcher was published last month.

k)   The organization plans to publish a new periodical, with three issues a year.

l)   Despite plans for economic growth of five per cent over the next year, unemployment is continuing to rise.

m)   We will need to modify the design of the equipment after a number of weaknesses were discovered in the testing process.

n)   Professor Jones is a leading authority on 17th-century Italian literature.

o)   The residential areas of the new town will be located well away from the industrial and commercial zones.

⊕CD1, Track 24

Ex 4.1
Listen to the following examples.

possess	possession	possessive
persuade	persuasion	persuasive
assess	assessment	assessed

However, in some cases the word stress may vary from one form to another. For example:

analyze, analysis, analytical

⊕CD1, Track 25

Ex 4.2
Listen and repeat these words. Mark the stressed syllable. The first one is done for you.

apply	application	applicable
activate	activity	active
inform	information	informative
-	probability	probable
socialize	society	social
experiment	experiment	experimental
equal	equality	equal
unite	union	united
transfer	transfer	transferable

⊕CD1, Track 26

Ex 4.3
Listen to these examples.

occur	occurrence
assume	assumption

⊕CD1, Track 27

Ex 4.5
Listen to the sentences and correct any that you got wrong.

Example: We need to analyze the data.

Statistical analysis of the data provided some unexpected results.

You need good analytical skills for this kind of work.

1   The stomach produces acids, which help to digest food.

The new model should be in production in November.

If the factory does not become more productive, it faces closure.

The product was withdrawn from sale after a number of defects were identified.

2   Four alternative methods of payment are offered.

She takes a very methodical approach to her work.

They have been developing a new method for research in this area.

3   The president stated that economic development was the main priority.

The chancellor is concerned that the economy is overheating.

She is studying economics at Lancaster University.

4   Wages tend to be higher in the private sector.

This law is intended to protect people's privacy.

The water services industry was privatized in the 1980s.

5   The heights of plants varied from 8 cm to 15 cm.

A wide variety of fruit is grown on the island.

Regional variations in the unemployment rate are significant.

A number of variables, such as wind speed and direction, humidity and air pressure, need to be considered.

6   Both approaches yielded similar results.

There are many similarities between the two religions.

The firefighters resorted to industrial action to settle the dispute. Similarly, railway workers are threatening to strike because of changes in working practices.

Unit 2 Summary

⊕CD1, Track 28

Ex 1
Listen to the words in the box. Then match them to the phonemic transcriptions below.

other   ankle   pull   shot   uncle   pool
short   another

Unit 3: Consonant sounds 1, sentence stress

⊕CD1, Track 29

Ex 1.1
Listen and repeat these continuous sounds.

ssssssssssssssss

zzzzzzzzzzzzzz

⊕CD1, Track 30

Ex 1.2
Listen and repeat each pair of words. Can you hear the difference in pronunciation?

pie	buy
town	down
coal	goal
sink	zinc
mesh	measure
chunk	junk
fast	vast
breath	breathe

⊕CD1, Track 31

Ex 1.3
Look at the following pairs of words and circle the word you hear.

Example: bill

a)   paste
b)   symbol
c)   dense
d)   try
e)   wide
f)   guard
g)   class
h)   angle
i)   zone
j)   price
k)   use (v)
l)   advise
m)   rich
n)   badge
o)   view
p)   prove
q)   belief

⊕CD1, Track 32

Ex 1.4
Listen and complete these sentences or phrases.

a) **1** a tense situation
   2 a dense material

b) **1** a wide area
   2 as white as a sheet

c) **1** at the base of the plant
   2 the pace of change

d) **1** Public services have improved.
   2 A cube has six surfaces.

e) **1** difficult to refuse
   2 It's had good reviews.

f) **1** the cause of the fire
   2 It changed the course of his life.

⊕CD1, Track 33

Ex 2.1
Listen to the difference in pronunciation between these pairs of words.

thing	sing
path	pass
worth	worse
mouth	mouse
youth	use

thin	tin
thank	tank
thread	tread
both	boat
death	debt

⊕CD1, Track 34

Ex 2.2
You will hear some of the words from Ex 2.1. Circle the phonemic transcription that matches the pronunciation of the word you hear.

Example: thin

a) tank
b) death
c) both
d) worth
e) pass
f) mouth
g) use

⊕CD1, Track 35

Ex 2.4
Now listen to the correct answers and repeat the sentences.

a) The painting is supposed to be worth five million pounds.
b) The fuel is stored in a 30-litre tank.
c) Cancer is the leading cause of death among women.
d) A thin layer of plastic is needed to provide waterproofing.
e) I couldn't follow the thread of his argument.
f) The thing is, no one likes to be criticized.
g) Tax increases are necessary to finance the national debt.

⊕CD1, Track 36

Ex 3.1
Listen and repeat these words.

the
this
these
that
those
they
their
there
theirs
than
then
though

⊕CD1, Track 37

Ex 3.2
Listen to these sentences and phrases and repeat them.

a) What's the weather like there?
b) Let's get together.
c) I'd rather not.
d) I wouldn't bother.
e) I don't like them.
f) I don't like them, either.
g) … further down the road …
h) … the other day …

⊕CD1, Track 38

Ex 4.1
Listen to these two words.

thank
than

CD1, Track 39

Ex 4.2
Listen to these phrases and write in the correct symbols above the words.

Example: ... another thing to consider is ...

a) ... in theory ...

b) ... the truth is that ...

c) ... the growth rate ...

d) ... a further theme ...

e) ... they thought that ...

f) ... this method ...

g) ... beneath the surface ...

h) ... this therapy might be used to ...

i) ... youth culture ...

CD1, Track 40

Ex 5.1
Listen to this recording of the previous paragraph.

While word stress (or accent) is generally decided by language rules, sentence stress (or prominence) is decided by speaker choice. The speaker usually chooses to stress content words, which carry the information, and not structure or function words, such as auxiliary verbs, pronouns, prepositions and determiners, although this is not always the case.

CD1, Track 41

Ex 5.2
Listen to these sentences, in which the sentence stress changes according to the meaning.

You have to hand in the essay on Monday ... there's a strict deadline.

You have to hand in the essay on Monday ... not the report.

You have to hand in the essay on Monday ... not Wednesday.

CD1, Track 42

Ex 5.3
Listen to these beginnings of sentences and choose the more suitable ending, according to the sentence stress.

a) Well, we know how this happened, ...

b) Having looked at the effect of deforestation on the environment, ...

c) Most of our cotton is imported, ...

d) The crime rate fell by 15 per cent last year, ...

e) The oil pump needs replacing, ...

CD1, Track 43

Ex 5.4
Now listen to the complete sentences to check your answers.

a) Well, we know how this happened, but do we know why it happened?

b) Having looked at the effect of deforestation on the environment, we will now discuss greenhouse gases and the roles they play.

c) Most of our cotton is imported, but we produce about 500,000 tonnes a year.

d) The crime rate fell by 15 per cent last year, but this year it's risen.

e) The oil pump needs replacing, not the filter.

CD1, Track 44

Ex 5.5
Read and listen to an extract from a lecture called *Introduction to British Agriculture*. Underline the words you hear stressed.

As a backdrop to all of these activities, particularly after the Second World War, a lot of effort was put into research and development of agriculture in terms of plant breeding, breeding crops that were higher yielding, that were perhaps disease-resistant, and so on and so forth. Also, crops that might have better quality, better bread-making quality, higher gluten content, to make them doughy, higher protein content, and so on and so forth. Research, too, and this is again at one of the university farms, research into livestock production. Understanding how to better manage our livestock, again to make them produce more, certainly, but also to produce and influence the quality of the livestock products, whether that happens to be milk or cheese, come back to that in a moment, or indeed meat.

CD1, Track 45

Ex 5.7
Read and listen to part of a lecture on globalization. Underline the words you hear stressed.

Now to get to the meat of the lecture, the basic purpose of this lecture is to give you some overview of the kind of contemporary academic and policy debate about globalization and particularly about a very specific, although rather general, debate itself, that is the debate on the effect of globalization on the role of the state. So, you see on the overhead, the lecture's going to be kind of in two parts: the first will be looking at globalization, causes and consequences, and more particularly a kind of definition of the discussion of some of the competing conceptions of globalization, that is, you know, what people say it is, so that we can then discuss in some detail, hopefully, this question of how globalization's affecting the state.

Unit 3 Summary

⊕CD1, Track 46

Ex 3
Listen and compare your ideas with the recording.

a) Some species of shark attack people, but most are harmless.
b) There used to be a Chemistry Department, but it closed in 2006.
c) The aid provided to the victims was too little, too late.
d) Many banks stopped lending, when the government wanted them to lend more.

Unit 4: Consonant sounds 2, word stress on two-syllable words

⊕CD1, Track 47

Ex 1.1
Listen to the pronunciation of the words in the box and write them under the correct heading.

decision

version

dimension

occasion

conclusion

discussion

expression

admission

expansion

supervision

confusion

erosion

⊕CD1, Track 48

Ex 1.2
Listen to the three different pronunciations of the word endings in the box and write them under the correct heading.

measure

pressure

closure

assure

ensure

pleasure

leisure

exposure

⊕CD1, Track 49

Ex 1.3
Listen and repeat the following words.

visual

casual

usually

sensual

⊕CD1, Track 50

Ex 2.1
Listen to and repeat the following words and phrases.

visit

develop

value

average

village

very good service

violent

every level

voice

When does it arrive?

⊕CD1, Track 51

Ex 3.1
The /ʝ/ sound appears at the beginning of words starting with y~. Listen and repeat.

yet

young

yellow

year

yesterday

⊕CD1, Track 52

Ex 3.2
The /ʝ/ sound also appears at the beginning of some words starting with u~. Tick the words below that are pronounced /ʝuː~/.

a) union
b) unless
c) uniform
d) uncle
e) unclear
f) unusual
g) useful
h) username
i) usual
j) uranium
k) until
l) urgent

⊙CD1, Track 53

Ex 3.3
You also find the /j/ sound in the middle of words, represented by y. Listen to these examples.

beyond

layer

layout

buyer

⊙CD1, Track 54

Ex 3.4
Sometimes, the /j/ sound in the middle of words is not represented by any character. Listen to these words and mark the position of the /j/ sound in them.

Examples:

new

continue

computer

a) fuel

b) view

c) argue

d) education

e) cube

f) few

g) rescue

h) distribute

i) assume

⊙CD1, Track 55

Ex 4.1
Listen to the difference in pronunciation between these pairs of words.

ship	chip
shop	chop
share	chair
shoes	choose
cash	catch
washed	watched
dishes	ditches

⊙CD1, Track 56

Ex 4.2
You will hear some of the words from Ex 4.1. Circle the phonemic transcription that matches the pronunciation of the word you hear.

Example: chop

a) catch

b) shoes

c) watched

d) share

e) ditches

f) chip

⊙CD1, Track 57

Ex 4.4
Listen to the correct answers and repeat the sentences.

a) There's a small chip on the card which stores your personal data.

b) You can pay with cash or by cheque.

c) Farmers need to dig ditches to drain the soil.

d) The share value has shot up by 30 per cent!

e) You can choose which topic to write about for your assignment.

f) The sample should be washed in a five per cent saline solution before analysis.

⊙CD1, Track 58

Ex 5.1
Listen to the difference in pronunciation between these pairs of words.

chunk	junk
cheap	Jeep
H	age
search	surge
rich	ridge
batch	badge

⊙CD1, Track 59

Ex 5.2
You will hear some of the words from Ex 5.1. Circle the phonemic transcription that matches the pronunciation of the word you hear.

Example: search

a) ridge

b) age

c) chunk

d) batch

e) Jeep

⊙CD1, Track 60

Ex 5.4
Listen to the correct answers and repeat the sentences.

a) Most fruit and vegetables are rich in vitamins.

b) Credit card bills are generally prepared by batch processing of data.

c) A large chunk of the budget is spent on overheads.

d) There is a ridge of high pressure running from north-west to south-east.

e) Children today eat too much junk food.

f) A sudden surge in the power supply can damage your computer.

Ex 6.1
Put the words into the correct column, according to their stress pattern.

provide

system

assist

reason

prepare

appear

recent

receive

include

certain

factor

question

problem

modern

suggest

reduce

private

observe

Ex 6.2
Listen to these pairs of sentences and underline the syllable that is stressed in the words in bold.

Example:

Coffee is this country's biggest export.

They export coffee mainly to Europe.

a) There has been a significant increase in unemployment.

It has been decided to increase the interest rate by a quarter of a per cent.

b) You need to keep a record of all the references you use in the essay.

She wants to record the lecture with her MP3 player.

c) About 30 people were present at the seminar.

He plans to present the results of his research at the conference.

Ex 6.4
Unlike the two-syllable words in Ex 6.3, the stress in words ending in ~er, ~ry, ~le, ~ion, ~age, ~ish, ~ow and ~us generally falls on the first syllable. Listen and repeat these words.

answer

gather

matter

suffer

angry

hurry

story

vary

angle

handle

middle

trouble

action

mention

nation

question

damage

language

manage

package

English

finish

publish

rubbish

follow

narrow

shadow

window

focus

minus

Unit 4 Summary

Ex 3
Listen to the following pairs of sentences, which contain words in bold with the same spelling. Mark the stressed syllable in each pair of words. For which pairs is the word stress the same, and for which is it different?

a) The contracts were signed last week.

The metal contracts as it cools down.

b) It caused a lot of damage.

How does it damage your health?

c) Why did they object to the proposal?

Archaeologists are not sure what this object was used for.

d) What is the main focus of your research?

We need to focus on the real issues.

Unit 5: Diphthongs 1, sounds in connected speech

Ex 1.1
Put the words in the box into the correct column, according to the pronunciation of the vowel or diphthong sound.

time
think
life
write
while
win
high
try
sit
site
buy
bit
might
sign
like

CD2, Track 2

Ex 1.3
How do you pronounce L-I-V-E in each of these sentences?

a) Where do you live?
b) The match is being shown live on TV.

CD2, Track 3

Ex 1.4
Listen to the six words below and complete the two activities.
a) Circle the phonemic transcription that matches the pronunciation of the word you hear.

1 while
2 fit
3 style
4 height
5 litter
6 hide

CD2, Track 4

Ex 1.5
Underline the /aɪ/ sounds in these sentences or phrases. Then listen and repeat them.

a) Try the other side.

b) The height's fine.
c) This type of plant needs a lot of light.
d) There was a slight rise in the share value.

CD2, Track 5

Ex 2.1
Put the words in the box into the correct column, according to the pronunciation of the vowel or diphthong sound.

cost
coast
show
rod
road
grow
lot
load
flow
hope
code
cold
not
note
fold

CD2, Track 6

Ex 2.3
Listen to the six words below and complete the activities.

a) Listen and circle the phonemic transcription that matches the pronunciation of the word you hear.

1 coast
2 not
3 rod
4 soak
5 won't
6 fond

CD2, Track 7

Ex 2.4
Underline the /əʊ/ sounds in these sentences or phrases. Then listen and repeat.

a) Most of the gold is exported.
b) … the hole in the ozone layer …
c) Gross profits were down.
d) Can you cope with the workload?

⊛CD2, Track 8

Ex 3.1
Put the words in the box into the correct column, according to the pronunciation of the vowel or diphthong sound.

plan

plane

dark

face

make

scale

large

lack

heart

play

weigh

gain

part

claim

bad

⊛CD2, Track 9

Ex 3.3
Listen to the eight words below and complete the activities.

a) Circle the phonemic transcription that matches the pronunciation of the word you hear.

    1 lack

    2 tape

    3 plan

    4 latter

    5 aim

    6 mark

    7 pace

    8 came

⊛CD2, Track 10

Ex 3.4
Underline the /eɪ/ sounds in these sentences or phrases. Then listen and repeat.

a) Can you explain this heavy rainfall?

b) That's quite a claim to make.

c) The future remains uncertain.

d) The failure rate is quite high.

⊛CD2, Track 11

Ex 4.1
Listen to these short conversations.

a) What do we need to solve the problem? A system.

b) What would you like me to do? Assist him.

⊛CD2, Track 12

Ex 4.2
Listen to the following examples.

hand in

split up

complex issue

⊛CD2, Track 13

Ex 4.3
Listen to these phrases and repeat them, linking the words together where this is indicated.

a) divide‿in two

b) historical‿evidence

c) as soon‿as possible

d) take‿over control

e) it'll‿end next week

f) the Data Protection‿Act

g) a wide‿area

h) keep‿up with‿it

i) an‿increase‿in crime

j) the main‿aim

⊛CD2, Track 14

Ex 4.4
Listen to this introduction from a talk about home ownership and write in the links between words.

In this presentation I'm going to talk about home ownership in the UK. First I'm going to focus on changes in the patterns of home ownership in the last 20 years and provide an explanation for these changes. Then I'm going to describe the process of buying or selling a house. Finally I'm going to try to make some predictions about the housing market.

⊛CD2, Track 15

Ex 4.6
Listen to the following examples.

slow economic growth

true identity

go up

⊛CD2, Track 16

Ex 4.7
Listen to the following examples.

carry on

high altitude

free access

⊕CD2, Track 17

Ex 4.8
Listen to the following examples.

aware of the problem

after all

faster access

⊕CD2, Track 18

Ex 4.9
Listen to these phrases and decide if a /w/, /j/ or /r/ sound needs to be inserted.

a) try out

b) agree on this

c) two of them

d) driver error

e) radio operator

f) media event

g) high above the Earth

h) How does this tie in?

Unit 5 Summary

⊕CD2, Track 19

Ex 1
Underline the diphthong sounds /aɪ/ in sentence (a), /əʊ/ in sentence (b) and /eɪ/ in sentence (c).

a) I think I'd like to carry on with Life Sciences, but I'm also interested in Psychology.
b) I want to go into social work, so I'm studying Sociology.
c) He came to Cardiff to give a paper on International Relations.

Unit 6: Consonant clusters 1, tone units 1

⊕CD2, Track 20

Ex 1.1
Listen and repeat these groups of words, which begin with consonant clusters.

blame
blind
blood

brand
break
brief

draw
draft
drop

platform
plenty
plus

practice
pressure
profit

transaction
trend
trigger

claim
climate
closure

create
crucial
criteria

quarter
quality
quota

glass
global
glue

graphics
ground
growth

twelve
twice
twin

flexible
flight
flow

fraction
freeze
frequent

threat
through
throw

shrink
shred

⊕CD2, Track 21

Ex 1.2
Listen and complete these sentences.

a) It burns with a blue flame.
b) There was a gradual rise in crime.
c) We are on track for ten per cent growth this year.
d) We need a more precise definition of the term.
e) It's covered with a steel plate.
f) The drum needs replacing.
g) Its development can be traced back to the 15th century.
h) The screen went blank.
i) There is fresh evidence for such a link.
j) It's difficult to follow the thread of his argument.

◉CD2, Track 22

Ex 1.4
Listen and repeat these further examples of consonant clusters which begin with /s/.

scale
scheme
scope
score

screen
script

snack
snow

sleep
slip
slight
slope

smart
smell
smoke
smooth

spare
spill
speed
spoil
specific

spray
spread
spring

split
splendid

stage
step
store
stuff
style

straight
stress
strike
strong

sweet
swing
switch

◉CD2, Track 23

Ex 1.5
Listen and complete these phrases or sentences.

a) This machine scans the brain.
b) Resources are scarce.
c) This species is under threat.
d) We're making slow progress.
e) one important strategy
f) He splashed paint on the floor.

g) a strange feeling
h) a bigger slice of the cake
i) in a stable condition
j) a stone floor

◉CD2, Track 24

Ex 2.1
Listen and repeat these words, which include consonant clusters.

impress
comprise
compromise

complain
complete
employ
sample

central
contract
control
entry
introduce

inspect
transport

explain
exploit
explore
explicit

extract
extreme

include
conclude
enclose
unclear

conflict
influence
inflation

abstract
construct
distribute
industry
illustrate

◉CD2, Track 25

Ex 2.2
Listen and complete these phrases or sentences with words from Ex 2.1.

a) Supplies need to be distributed.
b) no explicit reference
c) the transport infrastructure
d) this conflicts with
e) The causes are unclear.
f) oils extracted from plants
g) an abstract concept

h) in order to exploit its potential fully

i) It comprises three parts.

j) in extreme cases

⊕CD2, Track 26

Ex 3.1
Listen to these sentences and write in the word that is missing.

a) Did he tell you?

b) I've added her name to the list.

c) Can you put his suitcase in the car?

⊕CD2, Track 27

Ex 3.2
Listen and complete the sentences.

a) Although they've requested further funding, it's not certain that the project will continue beyond 2005.

b) The treatment is expensive, and that's why it's not very widely available.

c) Another advantage is that it'd lower the costs.

d) In fact, they're supposed to be checked every six months.

e) We can't know for sure, but it's thought that the space probe might've been hit by a meteorite.

f) Unfortunately, I'd forgotten just how complicated the process is.

g) The Vikings are believed to've landed in America well before Columbus.

h) The equipment testing shouldn't've been left until the last minute.

⊕CD2, Track 28

Ex 3.3
Listen to these words and phrases and, in the words in bold, cross out the vowels that are not pronounced.

a) Vegetables are grown on about 60 per cent of farms in the area.

b) Perhaps he's left.

c) Which category does it fit in?

d) She's studying medicine.

e) I'll phone her secretary.

⊕CD2, Track 29

Ex 3.4
Listen to the sentences a–f, paying particular attention to the consonant clusters in the words in bold. Cross out the consonants that are not pronounced.

a) It reacts with sulphur.

b) They'll send back the results on Tuesday.

c) It must be checked.

d) The low election turnout reflects growing apathy towards politics.

e) It has some good points.

f) The engine tends to overheat in particular circumstances.

⊕CD2, Track 30

Ex 4.1
Listen to someone speaking the above text and notice how it is split into tone units.

Whereas written English is split into words, spoken English is split into what are known as tone units. Each tone unit contains at least one prominent syllable. If, however, it contains two, then it is usually the second which contains the main sentence stress. This is the tonic syllable and it is where most of the pitch change takes place.

⊕CD2, Track 31

Ex 4.2
Listen to part of the lecture entitled *An Introduction to British Agriculture*. Mark the tone units by writing in double slash signs in the right places.

As a backdrop to all of these activities, particularly after the Second World War, a lot of effort was put into research and development of agriculture in terms of plant breeding, breeding crops that were higher yielding, that were perhaps disease-resistant, and so on and so forth.

Also, crops that might have better quality, better bread-making quality, higher gluten content to make them doughy, higher protein content, and so on and so forth.

Research, too, and this is again at one of the university farms, research into livestock production.

Understanding how to better manage our livestock, again to make them produce more, certainly, but also to produce and influence the quality of the livestock products, whether that happens to be milk or cheese, come back to that in a moment, or indeed meat.

⊕CD2, Track 32

Ex 4.3
Now listen to an extract from the lecture on globalization. Mark the tone units by writing in double slash signs in the right places.

Now to get to the meat of the lecture, the basic purpose of this lecture is to give you some overview of the kind of contemporary academic and policy debate about globalization and particularly about a very specific, although rather general debate itself, that is the debate on the effect of globalization on the role of the state. So you see on the overhead the lecture's going to be kind of in two parts: the first will be looking at globalization, causes and consequences and more particularly a kind of definition of the discussion of some of the competing conceptions of globalization, that is, you know, what people say it is, so that we can then discuss in some detail hopefully this question of how globalization's affecting the state.

Unit 6 Summary

⊕CD2, Track 33

Ex 1
Listen to how the following words are pronounced. Say the words in each group below. Underline any words that you find difficult to pronounce.

a) spare	spoil	speed	spray
b) central	entry	quarter	track
c) school	scale	share	scheme
d) street	store	stress	straight
e) complete	complex	construct	comprise
f) abstract	industry	construct	inspect

⊕CD2, Track 34

Ex 4
a) Listen to someone speaking the above text and mark the tone units.

You have got some interesting ideas and make some good points, but you could have developed these a bit more. You must make sure that you check your essay for spelling mistakes and check the grammar is correct. Perhaps you should have asked your tutor to read through your work, as he would have helped you improve it.

Unit 7 Diphthongs 2, tone units 2

⊕CD2, Track 35

Ex 1.1
Put the words in the box into the correct column of the table, according to the pronunciation of the diphthong sound.

share
fair
mere
square
near
adhere
sphere
year
there
where
aware
appear
severe
wear
pair
chair
bear
fare

⊕CD2, Track 36

Ex 1.3
Using words from Ex 1.1, complete these sentences by writing in the missing words.

a) As far as I'm aware, there has been little previous research into this issue.

b) Patients suffering from severe depression are often treated with drugs.

c) The mere fact that they have agreed to negotiate does not indicate that an end to the conflict is near.

d) These countries needed to prepare for entry into the EMU.

e) How can we repair the damage done?

f) The area of land is about 20 metres square.

g) The seeds adhere to the fur of animals, which distribute them over a large area.

h) We need to bear in mind that events in South America are largely beyond the UK's sphere of influence.

⊕CD2, Track 37

Ex 2.1
Put the words in the box into the correct column of the table, according to the pronunciation of *ow*.

allow
crowd
below
own
flow
down
power
growth
now
know
slow
follow
brown
show
powder
crown
owe
shower

CD2, Track 38

Ex 2.2
Underline the words below which include the /aʊ/ sound.

loud
doubt
group
account
court
serious
sound
various
trouble
south
amount
colour
course
enough
young
hour
ground
flavour

CD2, Track 39

Ex 2.3
Listen and complete the sentences, using words from Exs 2.1 and 2.2.

a) How do we account for this increase in temperature?
b) Margaret Thatcher came to power in 1979.
c) The new road system is designed to improve traffic flow through the city centre.
d) The animal feed is usually sold in powder form.
e) It is without doubt the most serious crisis the government has faced.
f) You need to allow 21 days for delivery.
g) Economic growth has slowed down over the last six months.
h) He is doing research into crowd behaviour.
i) A significant amount of water is lost through perspiration.
j) The cheese has quite a strong flavour.

CD2, Track 40

Ex 3.1
Listen and repeat the following words.

coin
point
join
avoid
soil

noise
boy
employ
enjoy
royal
annoy
soya

CD2, Track 41

Ex 3.2
Listen and complete these sentences by writing a word in each space.

a) The questionnaire comprises multiple-choice and open questions.
b) The government is keen for parents to have a voice in determining how their children are educated.
c) During the civil war, the army remained loyal to the king.
d) The company has appointed a new marketing director.
e) Large parts of the city were destroyed in the earthquake.
f) It is often claimed that we fail to exploit scientific developments made in UK universities.
g) Many sailors died during long sea voyages because of poor nutrition.
h) The new company is a joint venture between Italian and Egyptian oil companies.

CD2, Track 42

Ex 4.1
Listen and complete this lecture on higher education in England and Wales. Write one to five words in each space.

... in Britain, but in order to do that I'm going to tell you something about the education system before students get to the higher level. There are several reasons for this. One is, of course, it's part of the plan of your course designers to give you the experience of lectures before you go into your real departments in September or October, but another reason is that we have found in the past that many students come to Britain and they live and study here for a year or two and they go away without knowing some of the most basic facts about the education system here. It's also true that the education system here, perhaps as in your countries, is changing very rapidly, and this means that if you ask older people, you know, people as old as me, who don't actually have direct experience, they probably give you information about the education system as it used to be rather than as it actually is now.

Now what qualifications, as it were, do I have to speak on this particular subject? Well, I'm, as was said in the introduction, I'm here at Reading University and my main task is to look after international students here, like you, who need academic language support. Now between 20 and 23 per cent of the students in this university, in Reading University, do not have English as their first language and did not receive their previous education in the United Kingdom. So that's a large number of students, that's, you know, almost two and a half thousand students, in this university were not actually educated in the United Kingdom before they came to university, so you are amongst many. You are, you know, a minority, but you're a very large minority.

⊛CD2, Track 43

Ex 4.3
Listen to this excerpt from a lecture titled *Financial Markets and Instruments* and decide where the sentence stress falls.

Well, the title, *Financial markets and instruments*, what are we going to do here? Well, we're going to start by explaining why we need a financial market at all. What is the role that is played by a financial market? What is the rationale for having a financial market? And then we're going to move on and explain some of the instruments that are traded in those markets, some of the instruments that I was saying you are familiar with already, because they are simply stocks, bonds, bills: money market instruments. If you've done any finance before, you might be familiar also with the other ones, which are future swap options, which are derivative instruments, and I'm going to focus mainly on the stocks, bonds, bills, since these are by far the easiest to understand. OK, let's start with a simple definition, and I guess anyone here could have given this definition on their own: what is a financial market? Well, a financial market is a market where financial securities are traded. Nothing very very tricky here.

Unit 7 Summary

⊛CD2, Track 44

Ex 1
Listen and check your answers.

annoy

square

crowd

growth

severe

soya

although

doubt

steer

owe

pair

south

bear

avoid

year

Unit 8: Consonant clusters 2, intonation

⊛CD2, Track 45

Ex 1.1
Listen and repeat these groups of words, which end with consonant clusters.

arrival
critical
external
financial
principal

assemble
resemble

impact
conflict
affect
abstract

range
arrange
change
challenge

criticism
mechanism
organism
tourism

eleven
given
govern
driven

depth
length
strength
width
wealth

branch
lunch
launch
bench

⊛CD2, Track 46

Ex 1.2
Listen to these phrases and sentences and write the missing words in the spaces.

a) in the initial stage

b) The job has some fringe benefits.

c) I've lost a bunch of keys.

d) a rather uneven surface

e) It was discussed at some length.

f) This is a key aspect of his work.

g) He's studying journalism at Leeds University.

h) They can't afford to take such a gamble.

i) the removal of investment controls

j) in the seventh grade

CD2, Track 47

Ex 1.3
Listen to the past verb forms in the box and put them in the correct column of the table, depending on the pronunciation of ~ed.

equipped

combined

involved

concluded

constructed

depended

developed

expressed

claimed

advised

arranged

adapted

lacked

finished

absorbed

CD2, Track 48

Ex 1.4
Listen to the following examples.

I watch television every night.

and

I watched television last night.

or

Many suppliers raise their prices in situations like this.

and

Many suppliers raised their prices when the exchange rate rose.

CD2, Track 49

Ex 1.5
Listen and repeat these phrases.

a) arranged at short notice

b) the team involved in the project

c) it was constructed in three months

d) it's absorbed into the bloodstream

e) the benefits claimed in the report

f) we've avoided the problem

g) a technique developed in Brazil

h) specially adapted equipment

i) aimed at a niche market

j) enclosed in plastic

CD2, Track 50

Ex 2.1
Listen to the following short exchange.

A: Has everything been checked?

B: Yes, I think so.

A: What about the temperature?

B: Yes, I've checked the temperature, and it's normal.

Listen to the two words in isolation.

A: temperature

B: temperature

CD2, Track 51

Ex 2.2
Listen to another short exchange and do the three activities below.

A: It's too expensive.

B: Well, it's expensive, but it's worth it.

CD2, Track 52

Ex 2.3
Compare this conversation with the previous one.

A: It's too expensive.

B: Yes, it's a lot of money, but it's worth it.

CD2, Track 53

Ex 2.4
Listen to these short conversations. Notice the falling intonation for new information and the rising tone for information that is not new.

a) A: When's the deadline for the new building project?

B: The deadline? I think it's next Thursday.

b) A: Why do these prices fluctuate?

B: Changes in the exchange rate cause this variation.

CD2, Track 54

Ex 2.5
Listen to this conversation and mark the falling and rising intonation.

A: Can I help you?

B: Yes, where's the Physics Department?

A: It's on the second floor.

B: On the second floor?

A: Yes, that's right. Take the lift over there.

B: I'm not keen on lifts. I'd rather walk there.

A: Suit yourself. The stairs are down the corridor, on the left.

B: Down there, on the left. Thanks very much!

⊚CD2, Track 55

Ex 2.7
Listen to this short extract from a lecture and think about the use of intonation.

In these two lectures, we're going to look at two theories of child development. Firstly, I'm going to look at Jean Piaget. Then, next week, I'll talk about the life and work of Erick Erickson. So this week, it's about Jean Piaget. Now, Piaget's theories were very much influenced by his own experiences, so I'm going to talk about his life and how he developed his ideas, and then I'm going to describe Piaget's four stages of child development.

⊚CD2, Track 56

Ex 2.9
Listen to a student talking about the advantages and disadvantages of streaming video from a website and mark the rising and falling tones on the stressed words in bold.

With streaming video, the video is downloaded to your computer as you are listening to it. And usually you can't save it.

This stops people making copies of the video, editing or pirating it.

The problem is, if you don't have enough bandwidth, or if you're on a network and it's very busy, your computer won't be able to download fast enough.

As a result, the picture quality is often poor, or the pictures are jerky. Sometimes, the video even freezes.

⊚CD2, Track 57

Ex 2.12
Listen again to the first dialogue in Ex 2.1.
A: Has everything been checked?
B: Yes, I think so.

Consider also:
A: He's an excellent speaker.
B: I know what you mean.

⊚CD2, Track 58

Ex 2.13
Listen and compare the speakers' intonation in a) and b). Which one would you generally expect of an offer of help?
a) Can I help you?
b) Can I help you?

⊚CD2, Track 59

Ex 2.14
Finally, consider the function of the fall–rise in the following.
A: We need to improve the technology.
B: But training is just as important as technology.
A: That's just your opinion.
B: It's not just an opinion. There's evidence to support it.

Unit 8 Summary

⊚CD2, Track 60

Ex 2
Listen to the dialogue and mark the rising and falling tones on the stressed words marked in bold.
A: We need to discuss your essay. Can you come to my office at three o'clock?
B: I've got a lecture at three o'clock. And I think I'm working in the evening.
A: How about tomorrow? I'll be there at lunchtime.
B: OK. I'll come then.

Answer key

Unit 1: Vowel sounds 1, word stress and weak forms

Ex 1.2

a) /pɑːk/
b) /tɜːn/
c) /mæs/
d) /hiːt/
e) /wɜːnt/
f) /diːp/
g) /hed/
h) /hɑːt/
i) /bænd/

Ex 1.3

1 /sɪt/ sit	/siːt/ seat
2 /mæt/ mat	/met/ met
3 /hɜːt/ hurt	/hɑːt/ heart
4 /fɑː/ far	/fɜː/ fur
5 /lɪv/ live	/liːv/ leave
6 /sæd/ sad	/sed/ said

Ex 2.2

a) spe•cific (3)
b) al•ter (2)
c) re•source (2)
d) pre•lim•in•ary (5)
e) a•vail•a•ble (4)
f) con•se•quent (3)
g) frame•work (2)
h) sig•nif•ic•ant (4)
i) a•dapt (2)
j) dif•fer•en•ti•ate (5)

Ex 3.2

a) spe'cific
b) 'alter
c) re'source
d) pre'liminary
e) a'vailable
f) 'consequent
g) 'framework
h) sig'nificant
i) ad'apt
j) diffe'rentiate

Ex 3.3

a) pro'tection; 'purpose
b) 'analyzed
c) an'alysis
d) i'dentify; 'factors
e) peri'odicals
f) adminis'tration
g) per'centage
h) pro'cedure

Ex 4.1

In general, the underlined words (function words) are unstressed in sentences, and so they are pronounced with the /ə/ sound. Sometimes they are stressed, in which case they are pronounced with their full, strong form.

a) 1 /ə/ is unstressed (weak form)
   2 /ɑː/ is stressed (strong form)
b) 1 /səm/ is unstressed (weak form)
   2 /sʌm/ is stressed (strong form)
c) 1 /frɒm/ is stressed (strong form)
   2 /frəm/ is unstressed (weak form)
d) 1 /jɔː/ is stressed (strong form)
   2 /jə/ is unstressed (weak form)

Ex 4.2

a) at; of
b) at
c) have
d) for
e) than
f) as; for
g) can; at
h) of

Ex 4.3

Well, as Ros said, I'm going to talk about globalization today, which is one <u>of</u> the catch phrases or buzzwords, if you like, <u>of</u> the late 20th <u>and</u> early 21st centuries. It's constantly in <u>the</u> news. It's used by politicians, by people in <u>the</u> media, by business people, and when they're referring <u>to</u> globalization they talk about things like <u>the</u> way we <u>can</u> communicate almost instantaneously nowadays with people on the other side <u>of the</u> world by e-mail or by television. They're also talking about, <u>for</u> example, the way that <u>a</u> fall in share prices in one part <u>of the</u> world, <u>for</u> example in the Far East, <u>can</u> have an immediate impact on the stock markets on the other side <u>of the</u> world, like in London <u>or</u> Frankfurt.

Ex 4.4

a) past <u>and</u> present figures
b) more <u>or</u> less fifty
c) they were selected <u>at</u> random
d) it was far <u>from</u> clear

e) the results <u>of the</u> trials
f) too good <u>to</u> be true
g) needless <u>to</u> say
h) it's gone <u>from</u> bad <u>to</u> worse
i) we'll have <u>to</u> wait <u>and</u> see
j) we had <u>some</u> problems

Summary answers

Exs 1 and 2
a) two-syllable words: re'fer 'market
b) three-syllable words: 'century 'constantly 'media fi'nancial
c) four-syllable words: poli'tician
d) five-syllable words: globali'zation

Ex 3
/ɪ/ politician
/iː/ media
/e/ century
/ɜː/ refer
/æ/ financial
/ɑː/ market

Ex 4
a) Globalization is one <u>of the</u> buzzwords <u>of the</u> twenty-first century.
b) It's constantly in <u>the</u> news <u>and</u> is often referred to by politicians <u>and the</u> media.
c) <u>A</u> fall in share prices in one part <u>of the</u> world <u>can</u> have <u>an</u> impact on <u>the</u> stock markets on the other side <u>of the</u> world.

Ex 5
a) Why do you think learners confuse some of the vowel sounds you have practised in this unit? *Students may have fewer vowel sounds in their own language and be unable to differentiate between some English vowels.*
b) Why is it useful to make a note of the stressed syllable when you learn a new multi-syllable word? *It will help you remember the stress pattern. You can refer back to your notes if you forget how a word is stressed.*
c) How can you check the correct stress and number of syllables of words that you learn in English? *You can check in a good learners' dictionary.*

Unit 2: Vowel sounds 2, word stress patterns

Ex 1.2
a) /bʊks:/ books
b) /puːl/ pool
c) /spɪt/ spit
d) /mætʃ/ match
e) /ʌnkəl/ uncle
f) /fuːl/ fool
g) /lʌk/ luck
h) /stɒk/ stock
i) /ʃɔːt/ short

Ex 1.3
1 /fæn/ fan /fʌn/ fun
2 /muːd/ mood /mʌd/ mud
3 /kuːl/ cool /kɔːl/ call
4 /buːt/ boot /bɔːt/ bought
5 /fʊt/ foot /fuːd/ food
6 /kʊd/ could /kɑːd/ card

Ex 2.2
1 af'fect
2 'several
3 'standard
4 'failure
5 'purpose
6 pro'pose
7 'author
8 at'tempt
9 'distance
10 ac'cept
11 'opposite
12 'flavour
13 com'pare
14 ap'proach

Ex 2.4
1 in'vited
2 de'cision
3 de'mand
4 be'yond
5 ex'tensive
6 re'search
7 in'terpret

Ex 3.2
1 aca'demic
2 di'mension
3 bene'ficial
4 simi'larity
5 ma'jority
6 in'itial
7 de'mography
8 al'lergic
9 tra'dition
10 de'ficiency
11 con'ventional
12 'justify

Ex 3.3
a) optional
b) decision
c) definition
d) potential
e) solution
f) artificial
g) clarify
h) consortium
i) vacancy
j) biography
k) periodical
l) economic
m) modify
n) authority
o) residential

Ex 4.2

Verb	Noun	Adjective
ap'ply	appli'cation	ap'plicable
'activate	ac'tivity	'active
in'form	infor'mation	in'formative
–	proba'bility	'probable
'socialize	so'ciety	'social
ex'periment	ex'periment	experi'mental
'equal	e'quality	'equal
u'nite	'union	u'nited
trans'fer	'transfer	trans'ferable

Ex 4.4

1 pro'duction; pro'ductive; 'product
2 me'thodical; 'method
3 e'conomy; eco'nomics
4 'privacy; 'privatized
5 va'riety; vari'ations; 'variables
6 simi'larities; 'Similarly

Summary answers

Ex 1

a) /ənʌðə/ another
b) /puːl/ pool
c) /ʃɔːt/ short
d) /pʊl/ pull
e) /ʌŋkəl/ uncle
f) /æŋkəl/ ankle
g) /ʌðə/ other
h) /ʃɒt/ shot

Unit 3: Consonant sounds 1, sentence stress

Ex 1.3

a) paste
b) symbol
c) dense
d) try
e) wide
f) guard
g) class
h) angle
i) zone
j) price
k) use (v)
l) advise (v)
m) rich
n) badge
o) view
p) prove (v)
q) belief (n)

Exs 1.4 and 1.5

a) 1 tense U
    2 dense V
b) 1 wide V
    2 white U
c) 1 base V
    2 pace U
d) 1 services V
    2 surfaces U
e) 1 refuse U
    2 reviews V
f) 1 cause V
    2 course U

Ex 2.2

a) /tænk/ tank
b) /deθ/ death
c) /bəʊθ/ both
d) /wɜːθ/ worth
e) /pɑːs/ pass
f) /maʊθ/ mouth
g) /juːs/ use

Ex 2.3

a) worth
b) tank
c) death
d) thin
e) thread
f) thing
g) debt

Ex 4.2

a) … in theory
b) … the truth is that …
c) … the growth rate …
d) … a further theme …
e) … they thought that …
f) … this method …
g) … beneath the surface …
h) … this therapy might be used to …
i) … youth culture …

Ex 5.3

a) Well, we know how this happened, <u>but do we know why it happened?</u>
b) Having looked at the effect of deforestation on the environment, <u>we will now discuss greenhouse gases and the roles they play.</u>
c) Most of our cotton is imported, <u>but we produce about 500,000 tonnes a year.</u>
d) The crime rate fell by 15 per cent last year, <u>but this year it's risen.</u>
e) The oil pump needs replacing, <u>not the filter.</u>

Ex 5.5

As a <u>backdrop</u> to <u>all</u> of these activities, <u>particularly</u> after the Second World <u>War</u>, a lot of <u>effort</u> was put into <u>research</u> and <u>development</u> of <u>agriculture</u> in terms of <u>plant</u> breeding, breeding crops that were higher <u>yielding</u>, that were perhaps <u>disease</u>-resistant, and <u>so</u> on and <u>so</u> forth. <u>Also</u>, <u>crops</u> that might have better <u>quality</u>, better <u>bread</u>-making quality, higher <u>gluten</u> content, to make them <u>doughy</u>, higher <u>protein</u> content, and <u>so</u> on and <u>so</u> forth. <u>Research</u>, <u>too</u>, and this is again at one of the <u>university</u> farms, research into <u>livestock</u> production. Understanding how to better <u>manage</u> our livestock, again to make them <u>produce</u> more, certainly, but <u>also</u> to <u>produce</u> and <u>influence</u> the <u>quality</u> of the livestock <u>products</u>, whether that happens to be <u>milk</u> or <u>cheese</u>, come <u>back</u> to that in a moment, or indeed <u>meat</u>.

Ex 5.7

<u>Now</u> to get to the <u>meat</u> of the <u>lecture</u>, the <u>basic</u> purpose of this <u>lecture</u> is to <u>give</u> you some <u>overview</u> of the kind of <u>contemporary</u> academic and <u>policy</u> debate about <u>globalization</u> and <u>particularly</u> about a very <u>specific</u>, although rather <u>general</u>, debate itself, that is the <u>debate</u> on the effect of <u>globalization</u> on the role of the <u>state</u>. So, you see on the <u>overhead</u>, the lecture's going to be <u>kind</u> of in two <u>parts</u>: the <u>first</u> will be looking at <u>globalization</u>, <u>causes</u> and <u>consequences</u>, and more <u>particularly</u> a kind of <u>definition</u> of the <u>discussion</u> of some of the <u>competing</u> <u>conceptions</u> of <u>globalization</u>, <u>that</u> is, you know, what people say it <u>is</u>, so that we can then <u>discuss</u> in some <u>detail</u>, <u>hopefully</u>, this <u>question</u> of how <u>globalization's</u> affecting the <u>state</u>.

Summary answers

Ex 1

a) lose/loose, proof/prove, surge/search, three/free, very/ferry, seem/theme

Ex 3

a) <u>Some</u> species of shark attack people, but <u>most</u> are harmless.
b) There <u>used</u> to be a Chemistry Department, but it <u>closed</u> in 2006.
c) The aid provided to the victims was too <u>little</u>, too <u>late</u>.
d) Many banks <u>stopped</u> lending, when the government wanted them to lend <u>more</u>.

Ex 4

c) How is it helpful to study the phonemic symbols for different sounds?
If you learn the phonemic symbols you will be able to check the pronunciation of any word in a learner's dictionary that includes phonemic description of words.

d) Why is it helpful to be more aware of stressed words in a sentence?
Stressed words carry the new or important information of the utterance.

Unit 4: Consonant sounds 2, word stress on two-syllable words

Ex 1.1

/~ʒən/	/~ʃən/
decision	dimension
version	discussion
occasion	expression
conclusion	admission
supervision	expansion
confusion	
erosion	

Patterns:

When the spelling is vowel sound + ~*sion*, the word is pronounced /~ʒən/.

When the spelling is ~*nsion* or ~*ssion*, the word is pronounced /~ʃən/.

Ex 1.2

/~ʒə/	/~ʃə/	/~ʃɔː/
measure	pressure	assure
leisure		ensure
pleasure		
exposure		
closure		

Patterns:

When the spelling is vowel + ~*sure*, the word is pronounced /~ʒə/.

When the spelling is ~*nsure* or ~*ssure*, the word is pronounced /~ʃə/ or /~ʃɔː/.

Ex 3.2

a) union
c) uniform
g) useful

h) username
i) usual
j) uranium

Ex 3.4

a) fⁱuel
b) vⁱiew
c) argⁱue
d) edⁱucation
e) cⁱube
f) fⁱew
g) rescⁱue
h) distribⁱute
i) assⁱume

Ex 4.2

a) /kætʃ/ catch
b) /ʃuːz/ shoes
c) /wɒtʃt/ watched
d) /ʃeə/ share
e) /dɪtʃɪz/ ditches
f) /tʃɪp/ chip

Ex 4.3

a) chip
b) cash
c) ditches
d) share
e) choose
f) washed

Ex 5.2

a) /rɪdʒ/ ridge
b) /eɪdʒ/ age
c) /tʃʌnk/ chunk
d) /bætʃ/ batch
e) /dʒiːp/ Jeep

Ex 5.3

a) rich
b) batch
c) chunk
d) ridge
e) junk
f) surge

Ex 6.1

Oo	oO
question	provide
system	assist
reason	prepare
recent	appear
certain	receive
factor	include
problem	suggest
modern	reduce
private	observe

Ex 6.2

a) a significant 'increase; in'crease the interest rate
b) keep a 'record; re'cord the lecture
c) 30 people were 'present; pre'sent the results

Ex 6.3

Rules for word stress in two-syllable words:

Most two-syllable <u>nouns</u> and <u>adjectives</u> have stress on the first syllable.

Most two-syllable <u>verbs</u> have stress on the second syllable.

Summary answers

Ex 1

/ʃ/	/tʃ/	/dʒ/	/ʒ/
innovation	choices	suggest	confusion
distribution	watched	average	unusual

Ex 2

/v/ innovation, average and service
/j/ confusion, distribution and unusual

Ex 3

a) The 'contracts were signed last week.
   The metal con'tracts as it cools down.
b) It caused a lot of 'damage.
   How does it 'damage your health?
c) Why did they ob'ject to the proposal?
   Archaeologists are not sure what this 'object was used for.
d) What is the main 'focus of your research?
   We need to 'focus on the real issues.

Unit 5: Diphthongs 1, sounds in connected speech

Ex 1.1

/aɪ/	/ɪ/
time	think
life	win
write	sit
while	bit
high	
try	
site	
buy	
might	
sign	
like	

Ex 1.3

a) /lɪv/ (verb)
b) /laɪv/ (adverb, and also adjective)

Ex 1.4

1. /wɪl/ will   /waɪl/ while
2. /fɪt/ fit   /faɪt/ fight
3. /stɪl/ still   /staɪl/ style
4. /hɪt/ hit   /haɪt/ height
5. /lɪtə/ litter   /laɪtə/ lighter
6. /hɪd/ hid   /haɪd/ hide

Ex 1.5

a) Try the other side.
b) The height's fine.
c) This type of plant needs a lot of light.
d) There was a slight rise in the share value.

Ex 2.1

/əʊ/	/ɒ/
coast	cost
show	rod
road	lot
grow	not
load	
flow	
hope	
code	
cold	
note	
fold	

Ex 2.3

1. /kɒst/ cost   /kəʊst/ coast
2. /nɒt/ not   /nəʊt/ note
3. /rɒd/ rod   /rəʊd/ road
4. /sɒk/ sock   /səʊk/ soak
5. /wɒnt/ want   /wəʊnt/ won't
6. /fɒnd/ fond   /fəʊnd/ phoned

Ex 2.4

a) Most of the gold is exported.
b) … the hole in the ozone layer …
c) Gross profits were down.
d) Can you cope with the workload?

Ex 3.1

/eɪ/	/ae/	/ɑː/
plane	plan	dark
face	lack	large
make	bad	heart
scale		part
play		
weigh		
gain		
claim		

Ex 3.3

1. /læk/ lack   /leɪk/ lake
2. /tæp/ tap   /teɪp/ tape
3. /plæn/ plan   /pleɪn/ plane
4. /lætə/ latter   /leɪtə/ later
5. /ɑːm/ arm   /eɪm/ aim
6. /mɑːk/ mark   /meɪk/ make
7. /pɑːs/ pass   /peɪs/ pace
8. /kɑːm/ calm   /keɪm/ came

Ex 3.4

a) Can you explain this heavy rainfall?
b) That's quite a claim to make.
c) The future remains uncertain.
d) The failure rate is quite high.

Ex 4.4

In this presentation⌣I'm going to talk⌣about home ownership⌣in the UK. First I'm going to focus⌣ on changes in the patterns⌣of home ownership in the last 20 years and provide⌣an explanation for these changes. Then⌣I'm going to describe the process⌣of buying or selling⌣a house. Finally⌣I'm going to⌣try to make some predictions⌣about the housing market.

Ex 4.9

a) try /ʲ/ out
b) agree /ʲ/ on this
c) two /w/ of them
d) driver /r/ error
e) radio /w/ operator
f) media /r/ event
g) high /ʲ/ above the Earth
h) How does this tie /ʲ/ in?

Summary answers

Ex 1

a) I think I'd like to carry on with Life Sciences, but I'm also interested in Psychology. /aɪ/
b) I want to go into social work, so I'm studying Sociology. /əʊ/
c) He came to Cardiff to give a paper on International Relations. /eɪ/

Ex 2

a) I⌣think⌣I'd like to⌣carry⌣ʲ⌣on with Life Sciences, but⌣I'm also⌣w⌣interested⌣in⌣Psychology.
b) I⌣wan(t)⌣to⌣go⌣w⌣into⌣social work, so⌣w⌣I'm studying Sociology.
c) He⌣came to⌣Cardiff to⌣give⌣a⌣paper⌣r⌣on⌣International Relations.

98   English for academic study

Ex 3

carry on – /j/
go into – /w/
paper on – /r/

Ex 5

a) Learners may sometimes be misunderstood if they confuse vowel and diphthong sounds, but the meaning is usually clear from the context.
b) Learners will generally still be perfectly intelligible if they don't link words as native speakers do.

Unit 6: Consonant clusters 1, tone units 1

Ex 1.2

a)	flame	f)	drum
b)	gradual	g)	traced
c)	track; growth	h)	blank
d)	precise	i)	fresh
e)	plate	j)	thread

Ex 1.5

a)	scans	f)	splashed
b)	scarce	g)	strange
c)	species	h)	slice
d)	slow	i)	stable
e)	strategy	j)	stone

Ex 2.2

a)	distributed	f)	extracted
b)	explicit	g)	abstract
c)	transport	h)	exploit
d)	conflicts	i)	comprises
e)	unclear	j)	extreme

Ex 3.1

a) he
b) her
c) his

Ex 3.2

a) they've (they have); it's (it is)
b) that's (that is); it's (it is)
c) it'd (it would)
d) they're (they are)
e) can't (can not); it's (it is); might've (might have)
f) I'd (I had)

g) to've (to have)
h) shouldn't've (should not have)

Ex 3.3

a) Vegetables are grown on about 60 per cent of farms in the area.
b) Perhaps he's left.
c) Which category does it fit in?
d) She's studying medicine.
e) I'll phone her secretary.

Ex 3.4

a) It reacts with sulphur.
b) They'll send back the results on Tuesday.
c) It must be checked.
d) The low election turnout reflects growing apathy towards politics.
e) It has some good points.
f) The engine tends to overheat in particular circumstances.

Ex 4.2

As a backdrop to all of these activities, // particularly after the Second World War, // a lot of effort was put into research // and development of agriculture // in terms of plant breeding, // breeding crops that were higher yielding, // that were perhaps disease-resistant, // and so on and so forth. // Also, // crops that might have better quality, // better bread-making quality, // higher gluten content to make them doughy //, higher protein content, // and so on and so forth. // Research, too, // and this is again at one of the university farms, // research into livestock production. // Understanding how to better manage our livestock, // again to make them produce more, // certainly, // but also // to produce and influence // the quality of the livestock products, // whether that happens to be milk or cheese, // come back to that in a moment, // or indeed meat.

Ex 4.3

Now // to get to the meat of the lecture, // the basic purpose of this lecture // is to give you some overview // of the kind of contemporary academic // and policy debate // about globalization // and particularly about a very specific, // although rather general debate itself, // that is the debate on the effect of globalization // on the role of the state. // So // you see on the overhead // the lecture's going to be kind of in two parts: // the first will be looking at globalization, // causes and consequences // and more particularly // a kind of definition of the discussion // of some of the competing conceptions // of globalization, // that is, you know, // what people say it is // so that we can then discuss in some detail // hopefully // this question of how globalization's // affecting the state.

Summary answers

Exs 2 and 3

a) 'spray' is the odd one out. (It has the consonant cluster /spr/. The other words have the cluster /sp/.)

b) 'quarter' is the odd one out. (The other words have the cluster /tr/.)

c) 'share' is the odd one out. (It has the consonant sound /ʃ/. The other words have the cluster /sk/.)

d) 'store' is the odd one out. (It has the consonant cluster /st/. The other words have the cluster /str/.)

e) 'construct' is the odd one out. (It has four consonants, n + the cluster /str/. The other words have m + /pl/ or /pr/.)

f) 'inspect' is the odd one out. (It has the cluster /sp/. The other words have the cluster /skr/.)

Ex 4

You have got some **interesting ideas** // and make some **good points**, // but you could have **developed** these a bit more. // You **must** make **sure** // that you **check** your **essay** // for **spelling** mistakes // and **check** the **grammar** is correct. // Perhaps you should have **asked** your **tutor** // to read **through** your work, // as **he** would have helped you **improve** it. //

Unit 7: Diphthongs 2, tone units 2

Ex 1.1

/eə/	/ɪə/
share	mere
fair	near
square	adhere
there	sphere
where	year
aware	appear
wear	severe
pair	
chair	
bear	
fare	

Ex 1.3

a) aware **e)** repair

b) severe **f)** square

c) mere **g)** adhere

d) prepare **h)** bear; sphere

Ex 2.1

/aʊ/	/əʊ/
allow	below
crowd	own
down	flow
power	growth
now	know
brown	slow
powder	follow
crown	show
shower	owe

Ex 2.2

loud	south
doubt	amount
group	colour
account	course
court	enough
serious	young
sound	hour
various	ground
trouble	flavour

Ex 2.3

a) account **f)** allow

b) power **g)** growth

c) flow **h)** crowd

d) powder **i)** amount

e) doubt; serious **j)** flavour

Ex 3.2

a) choice **e)** destroyed

b) voice **f)** exploit

c) loyal **g)** voyages

d) appointed **h)** joint; oil

Exs 4.1 and 4.2

... in Britain, // but in order to do that // I'm going to tell you something about the education system // before students get to the higher level. // There are several reasons for this. // One is, // of course, // it's part of the plan of your course designers // to give you the experience of lectures // before you go into your real departments // in September or October, // but another reason is that we have found in the past // that many students come to Britain // and they live and study here for a year or two // and they go away without knowing // some of the most basic facts about the education system here. // It's also true // that the education system here, // perhaps as in your countries, // is changing very rapidly, // and this means // that if you ask older people, // you know, people as old as me, // who don't <u>actually</u> have direct <u>experience</u>, // they probably give you information about the education system // as <u>it used to be</u> // rather than as it <u>actually</u> is now.

Now // what qualifications, // <u>as it were</u>, // do I have // to speak on this particular <u>subject</u>? // Well, I'm, // <u>as was said</u> in the introduction, // I'm here at Reading University // and my main <u>task</u> is to look after international students here // like you // who need academic language support. // Now between 20 and 23 percent // of the students in this university, // in Reading University, // do not have English as their first language // and did not receive their previous education // in the United Kingdom. // So that's a large number of students, // <u>that's, you know</u>, // almost two and half thousand students, // in this university // were not <u>actually</u> educated // in the United Kingdom before they came to university, // so you are amongst many. // <u>You are</u>, // <u>you know</u>, // a minority, // but you're a very large minority.

Exs 4.3 and 4.4

Well, the <u>title</u>, // *Financial markets and instruments*, // what are we going to <u>do</u> here? // Well, // we're going to <u>start</u> by explaining // why we need a financial market at <u>all</u>. // What is the <u>role</u> // that is <u>played</u> by a financial market? // What is the rationale // for having a financial market? // And then we're going to <u>move</u> on and explain // some of the <u>instruments</u> // that are <u>traded</u> in those <u>markets</u>, // some of the <u>instruments</u> // that I was <u>saying</u> you are familiar with already, // because they are simply <u>stocks</u>, // <u>bonds</u>, // <u>bills</u>: // money market <u>instruments</u>. // If you've done any finance be<u>fore</u>, // you might be familiar <u>also</u> // with the other ones, // which are future swap <u>options</u>, // which are derivative <u>instruments</u>, // and I'm going to focus <u>mainly</u> // on the <u>stocks</u>, // <u>bonds</u>, // <u>bills</u>, // since <u>these</u> are by far the <u>easiest</u> to understand. // OK, let's start with a simple definition, // and I guess <u>anyone</u> <u>here</u> could have given // <u>this</u> definition on their <u>own</u>: // What is a financial <u>market</u>? // Well, a financial market is a <u>market</u> // where financial securities are <u>traded</u>. // <u>Nothing</u> very very tricky <u>here</u>. //

Summary answers

Ex 1

/eə/	bear	square	pair
/ɪə/	severe	year	steer
/aʊ/	crowd	doubt	south
/əʊ/	owe	growth	although
/ɔɪ/	avoid	annoy	soya

Ex 3

steer /stɪə/ and although /ɔːlðəʊ/ are exceptions to the patterns you looked at in the unit.

Unit 8: Consonant clusters 2, intonation

Ex 1.2

a) initial

b) fringe

c) bunch

d) uneven

e) length

f) aspect

g) journalism

h) gamble

i) removal

j) seventh

Ex 1.3

/t/ or /d/	/ɪd/
equipped	concluded
combined	constructed
involved	depended
developed	adapted
expressed	
claimed	
advised	
arranged	
lacked	
finished	
absorbed	

Ex 2.2

A: It's too ↓expensive.

B: Well, it's expensive, but it's ↓worth it.

Ex 2.5

A: Can I ↑help you?

B: Yes, where's the ↓Physics Department?

A: It's on the second ↓floor.

B: On the ↑second floor?

A: Yes, that's right. Take the ↓lift over there.

B: I'm not keen on ↑lifts. I'd rather ↓walk there.

A: Suit yourself. The ↓stairs are down the ↓corridor, on the ↓left.

B: ↑Down there, on the ↓left. Thanks very much!

Ex 2.9

With ↓streaming video, the video is ↓downloaded to your ↓computer as you are ↓listening to it, and usually you can't ↓save it.

This ↓stops people making ↓copies of the video, ↓editing or ↓pirating it. The ↑problem is, if you don't have enough ↑bandwidth, or if you're on a ↑network and it's very ↑busy, your ↓computer won't be able to download ↓fast enough.

As a ↑result, the picture quality is often ↑poor, or the pictures are ↑jerky. Sometimes, the video even ↓freezes.

Summary answers

Ex 1

Possible answers: allow variations
- Sometimes, consonant sounds can disappear when *it becomes too difficult to pronounce them all in a cluster in connected speech, e.g., in 'This used to cause problems', the d normally disappears.*

- *-ed* past forms of regular verbs can be pronounced in three different ways: /d/, /t/, /ɪd/, *depending on the ending (sound) of the verb, e.g., finished /t/, combined /d/, depended /ɪd/.*

- If you find consonant clusters difficult to pronounce, try *linking the final consonant to the following word.*

Ex 2

A: We need to discuss your ↓**essay**. Can you come to my office at ↓**3.00**?
B: I've got a lecture at ↑**3.00**. And I think I'm working in the ↓**evening**.
A: How about ↓**tomorrow**? I'll be there at ↓**lunchtime**.
B: OK. I'll come ↑**then**.